MW00334464

German Touches

Recipes and Traditions

German-American Life: Revised and Expanded

Cincinnati USA Regional Chamber photo

Children in folk costumes celebrate Oktoberfest Zinzinnati.
In 1840, half of Cincinnati's population was German.

By Mary Sharp

Acknowledgments

Front cover:

Otto Martin, age 3, is wearing a homemade *Sepplhut,* a type of typical Bavarian felt hat and *Lederhosen. Sepplhut* come in a variety of styles, some pointed and others floppy. *Photo by his mother, Jessica Martin.*

Back cover:

Maifest, Amana, Iowa, Allison Momany and Emilie Trumpold
Emilie Hoppe photo

Helen, Georgia *Greater Helen Area Chamber of Commerce photo*

Leavenworth, Washington *Joan Liffring-Zug Bourret photo*

Apple Struedel *The Berghoff Restaurant photo, Chicago, Illinois*

For this book, Mary Sharp updated sections of *German-American Life: Recipes and Traditions,* published in 1990 by Penfield Press.

Cover design by: MACook Design
Drawings by: Diane Heusinkveld and Esther Feske
Edited by: Dwayne and Joan Liffring-Zug Bourret, Melinda Bradnan, Miriam Canter, Jacque Gharib, and Deb Schense. 1990 editors included John D. Zug, Karin Gottier, Marlene Domeier, and Dorothy Crum
Photo page 91 credit: "DSCN4624 holmescountyamishbuggy e". Licensed under Creative Commons Attribution-Share Alike 3.0 via Wikimedia Commons
http://commons.wikimedia.org/wiki/File:DSCN4624_holmescountyamishbuggy_e.jpg#mediaviewer/File:DSCN4624_holmescountyamishbuggy_e.jpg

In addition to those named in the book, we thank many contributors. They include: Cynthia Browne, Deutschheim Historic Site; Sister Bernardine Bichler, Rudolph C. Block, Lynn Hattery-Beyer, Arthur Canter, the Rev. Bill Eckhardt, Helen Kraus, Paul L. Maier, Harry Oster, Julie McDonald, Stephen Scott, Dianne Stevens, Anneliese Heider Tisdale, and the Harmony Museum and The Old Economy Village in Pennsylvania.

Library of Congress Control Number: 2014931556
© 1990 Penfield Press *German-American Life*
ISBN-13: 978-1932043907
© 2014 Penfield Books, 215 Brown Street, Iowa City, IA 52245
Printed in the U. S. A.
Phone: 1-319-337-9998   E-mail: penfield@penfieldbooks.com
Website: www.penfieldbooks.com

Contents

Dedication

For my grandson, Forrest Heusinkveld, a musician

Forrest's German ancestry comes from his maternal grandparents, the Amana Schmieders, Roemigs, and Oehls. From his paternal grandparents, his German ancestry comes from the Langs, Medders, and Hinrichs.

Joan Liffring-Zug Bourret
Publisher, Penfield Books

A Shared Heritage

What do fifty-two million Americans—and more than three million Canadians—have in common? German ancestors.

About seventeen percent of Americans claim German ancestry, making that heritage the largest of any group in the United States. Germans made up the largest, non-English-speaking group to settle in the United States.

The percentage of those with German heritage is highest in the Midwest, where close to one-third of the population claims that ancestry. California, Texas, and Pennsylvania have the largest number of people claiming German ancestry. And German is among the top five heritages in all the states except for two (Maine and Rhode Island).

Some of the German settlers came to the United States for religious or political freedom. But it was mainly land—cheap, plentiful land—that drew more than eight million German settlers to the United States and Canada in the nineteenth century.

All you have to do is look at a map to understand the allure. Three American states—Texas, California, and Montana—are bigger than modern-day Germany. The Prairie Provinces in Canada offered the same vast expanses.

Plus, in Germany, as in all of Europe, it was common for the eldest son to inherit a family's estate, meaning younger children had to fend for themselves. Countless others saw the New World as a way to escape poverty and to support and feed their families—something they were unable to do in the Old World.

The United States government, in its infancy, had land but few people. It gave the railroads huge land grants, and the railroads, in turn, set up recruiting agencies in German cities, offering land, easy credit, and cheap transportation for those willing to leave behind the familiar for the new.

And so the rush began. Müllers, Schmidts, and Schneiders farmed the land, gave their names to cities and businesses, saved their money, and founded schools, churches, and gymnastic societies. Their Christmas trees, beers, and sausages became part of the America culture. And though their patriotism was questioned during two world wars with Germany, they endured and proved their loyalty, living to see a time when their heritage would once again be celebrated.

This book looks at this shared heritage and the resurgence of interest in all things German, including the opening of a new, national German-American Heritage Museum in Washington, D.C., in March 2010.

And what is a heritage without food? Hence: dozens of time-tested German recipes appear in the last section of this book. *Genießen—*enjoy!

Christoph Avril photo

The German-American Heritage Museum in Washington, D.C.

Getting ready to cut the ribbon to open the German-American Heritage Museum at 719 Sixth Street NW in Washington, D.C., on March 20, 2010, are (from left) Bern E. Deichmann, president of the German-American Heritage Foundation; U.S. Sen. Richard Lugar, R-Indiana; and Klaus Scharioth, German ambassador to the United States.

The museum's mission is to tell the impact of four hundred years of German immigration on the development of the United States. The exhibits tell the story of German immigration to and migration across the United States.

Germans in the New World

Norse sagas say the first German to set foot in the New World was Tyrker, Leif Ericson's foster father and a member of Ericson's thirty-five-man expedition to Newfoundland in 1001. Tyrker discovered wild grapes near the settlement, leading to a name for the new land—Vinland.

Captain John Smith recruited the hard-working Germans for the first English settlement in Jamestown, Virginia, in 1607. Dr. Johannes Fleischer was among that first group of settlers. A year later, five German glassmakers and three carpenters arrived.

Although Smith called the Germans "damned Dutch" because they wouldn't kowtow to the English "gentlemen," Smith asked authorities to send thirty Germans or Poles rather than a thousand Englishmen like the ones he had.

German settlement began in earnest when the *Concord,* sometimes called the *German Mayflower,* sailed to Philadelphia on October 6, 1683. Aboard were thirteen Mennonite families from Krefeld. Under the leadership of Franz Pastorius, a lawyer from Franconia, the families built Germantown about six miles from Philadelphia, the first distinctly German settlement in the Americas.

Germantown was part of William Penn's "Holy Experiment" to offer a refuge to Europeans fleeing from religious persecution. Penn, an aristocratic Quaker, lured settlers with effective marketing—cheap land, religious tolerance, and political freedom.

Pennsylvania and upstate New York were the preferred destinations for Germans until the mid-1700s. Most of the settlers were Lutherans, with German Catholics arriving in numbers in the 1800s. Others belonged to small sects like the Mennonites or Amish.

The largest early German migration came in 1710 when about two thousand Protestant refugees from the Palatinate region of Germany arrived in the Colonies via London. Most of them settled near New York City.

John Peter Zenger became the most famous of the Palatine immigrants. A newspaper editor, he led the fight for freedom of the press.

John Jacob Astor, who arrived in the States in the late 1700s, made a fortune in fur trading, buying and selling real estate, and developing property. He would become the richest man in America.

By the start of the American Revolution in 1776, some two hundred twenty-five thousand Germans were living in what would become the United States of America. The early arriving Germans included Hessians, soldiers hired by the king of England to fight the American revolutionaries. In 1776, the Continental Congress ordered a message printed on the back of all tobacco wrappers, offering each Hessian soldier fifty acres and American citizenship. After the war, five thousand to twelve thousand former Hessians stayed in the country they had come to fight.

In the 1800s, Germans moved on to settle in Texas, Ohio, Minnesota, North Carolina, Wisconsin, Nebraska, Iowa, California, Michigan, Virginia, Massachusetts, Georgia, and other states.

The fresh start appealed to Germans, who came from a land devastated by a series of wars. Efforts of both Protestants and Catholics to create "100 percent" pure areas also had been disruptive, and German military service was mandated—something that did not appeal to all.

The New World offered opportunity, where life could be lived outside some of the social structures of the Old World. In America, one could rise "from a servant to the rank of master," J. Hector St. John de Crèvecoeur wrote in his book, *Letters from an American Farmer.* Immigrants wrote home urging friends and family members to join them. Iowa and Wisconsin sent recruitment pamphlets for distribution in Germany.

Getting out of Germany was not easy. The bureaucracy required documents, including baptismal and marriage certificates, official evidence concerning business, profession, or trade, place of residence, name and places of birth of parents, a certified copy of an emigration certification from a government source, a certificate of good conduct from the congregations, and official information on the financial status of the immigrant.

The voyage itself presented dangers. Tightly packed onto ships, some passengers died of hunger, thirst, and disease during trips that could take up to several months. Some ships sank, though the sinkings were hushed up so as not to discourage passage.

Some immigrants paid their passage by promising to work for three to seven years as indentured servants. Some of those terms amounted to slavery. Conditions improved after 1819, when Congress passed laws limiting the number of passengers on a ship and allowing abused passengers to sue the captain.

Pennsylvania by 1775, was about one-third German. Many arrived as indentured servants and then turned to farming. A number would support the American Revolution in 1776, but others remained loyal to the English throne, fearing they would lose land titles or individual freedoms if they sided with colonists.

In Louisiana, about nine thousand Germans settled north of New Orleans in 1721 along the "German Coast."

In Virginia, Germans founded Germanna in 1714 near what is today Culpeper, Virginia.

Germans living in Pennsylvania bought land—near what is now Winston-Salem, North Carolina—in 1753 and founded the town of Salem in 1766 and Salem College, a college for women, in 1772.

An estimated one thousand Germans settled in Broad Bay, Massachusetts—now Waldoboro, Maine—between 1742 and 1753 but fled when native Indians burned homes and killed many of the settlers. Those remaining turned to fishing and shipping work rather than farming.

By 1790, about nine percent of the U.S. population was German, based on the analysis of names recorded in the census.

The greatest influx of German settlers came between 1815 and 1915, with nearly six million Germans immigrating to America, and a quarter of a million arriving in 1882 alone. Another major wave came in 1848—possibly as many as ten thousand—following the failed revolution in the German states. Those settlers became known as the "Forty-Eighters." Their numbers included highly educated intellectuals and professionals such as Carl Schurz, who, some suggested, could have been president had he been born in the United States.

About half of the nineteenth-century immigrants chose to farm, with the majority settling in the Midwest and Upper Plains. The Germans who'd earlier settled in Russia—until conscription and government policies persuaded many to move—headed for Kansas, Nebraska, and the Dakotas. As farmers, they specialized in raising sugar beets.

The other half of the German immigrants settled in cities like New York, Chicago, St. Louis, Milwaukee, and Cincinnati. By 1900, forty percent of those living in Cincinnati, Cleveland, and Milwaukee claimed German heritage. The percentage was even higher in Dubuque and Davenport, Iowa, and German Americans made up fifty-seven percent of the population of Omaha, Nebraska, in 1910.

Many Germans lived in the same area of cities, creating "Germantown" or Germania districts or, in Milwaukee, "the German Athens."

They worked as skilled craftsmen and in breweries, where German Americans founded the well-known brands of Blatz, Miller, Pabtz, and Schlitz.

Few Germans settled in the South, though Texas was an exception, with about twenty thousand Germans counted in the 1850 census. The settlements were primarily around Galveston and Houston.

When the American Civil War started in 1861, most German Americans were anti-slavery and joined the Union Army. The Germans were the largest immigrant group to participate in the Civil War, with one hundred seventy-six thousand Union soldiers born in Germany, according to B.A. Gould's 1869 study of soldier nativity. (The number of German Americans who became Confederate soldiers is not known, though it is assumed to be a small number.)

For the most part, German Americans were apolitical, and few ran for political office. This lack of political power likely was one of the reasons that anti-German sentiment gained such momentum during World War I, when the United States and its Allies were fighting Germany.

More than four thousand Germans were jailed in the United States after being determined to be pro-German or thought to be spies. Germans were forced to buy war bonds to prove their loyalty. It became politically incorrect to converse in German, with Iowa even banning foreign languages in schools and public places in 1918. Schools and churches quit using German. German books were banned. A number of German Americans anglicized their last names, with Schmidts becoming Smiths, Müllers becoming Millers.

The anti-German sentiment also weakened the German singing societies, whose performances had been major entertainment, and the Turner societies, which served as social clubs in German émigré communities. But the strength of such groups was already dying out, as younger German Americans melted into the English-speaking American mainstream.

After World War I, another one hundred fourteen thousand Germans immigrated to the United States, many of them Jews, including scientist Albert Einstein, fleeing the rise of Adolf Hitler and the Nazis in Germany.

With America's entry into World War II in December 1941, another wave of anti-German (and anti-Japanese) sentiment swept through the United States. German-born residents had to register with the government; some eleven thousand Germans were put in camps where their rights and ability to travel were restricted.

Nonetheless, many Americans of German descent were chosen for top jobs in the war, including Dwight D. Eisenhower, who would head all the Allied forces and coordinate the D-Day landing in Europe. Americans with German language skills were recruited for intelligence work and as translators during and after the war.

The last major groups of German immigrants to the United States came in the ten years after World War II—primarily displaced persons from Silesia, Prussia, Poland, Hungary, Yugoslavia, Slovakia, Czechoslovakia, Romania, and Russia. Many were scientists, former prisoners of war, and German war brides.

The United States and its Allies helped rebuild Germany after the war. With time, anti-German sentiment faded in the United States. German Americans were once again able to embrace their language, traditions, and heritage. With the fall of the Berlin Wall and the reunification of East and West Germany in 1990, travel to Germany also became more popular. By the twenty-first century, the unified Germany was among the most prosperous countries in Europe.

The impact of German Americans in the United States cannot be overstated. The heritage produced great generals—Eisenhower, John Pershing, Norman Schwarzkopf—and businessmen whose names are household words, among them John D. Rockefeller, Adolphus Busch, Walter Chrysler, Adolph Coors, Harvey Firestone, Henry E. Steinway, Joseph Schlitz, and George Westinghouse.

German Americans also took their place in the arts—Oscar Hammerstein, Theodore Dreiser, Kurt Vonnegut, Thomas Mann—and such celebrities as Fred Astaire, Lauren Bacall, Doris Day, Babe Ruth, Lou Gehrig, Jack Nicklaus, Arnold Schwarzenegger, and Leonardo DiCaprio.

German Ancestry by City and State

Here are the twenty U.S. communities with the highest percentage of residents claiming German ancestry. *Source: epodunk.com*

1. Monterey, Ohio 83.6%
2. Granville, Ohio 79.6%
3. St. Henry, Ohio 78.5%
4. Germantown Township in Illinois 77.6%
5. Jackson, Indiana 77.3%
6. Washington, Ohio 77.2%
7. St. Rose, Illinois 77.1%
8. Butler, Ohio 76.4%
9. Marion, Ohio 76.3%
10. Jennings, Ohio 75.6%
11. Germantown, Illinois 75.6%
12. Coldwater, Ohio 74.9%
13. Jackson, Ohio 74.6%
14. Union, Ohio 74.1%
15. Minster, Ohio 73.5%
16. Kalida, Ohio 73.5%
17. Greensburg, Ohio 73.4%
18. Aviston, Illinois 72.5%
19. Teutopolis, Illinois 72.4%
20. Cottonwood, Minnesota 72.3%

Here are the top ten U.S. states with the highest percentage of residents claiming German ancestry. *Source: http://en.wikipedia.org/wiki/German_American*

1. North Dakota 46.8%
2. Wisconsin 43.9%
3. South Dakota 44.5%
4. Nebraska 42.7%
5. Minnesota 38.4%
6. Iowa 35.7%
7. Montana 27.0%
8. Ohio 26.5%
9. Wyoming 25.9%
10. Kansas 25.8%

Germans in Canada

Germans began immigrating to Nova Scotia in the mid-1700s, as England recruited German-Protestant settlers in an effort to balance out the numerous Catholics.

Still more came after the Revolutionary War in the United States, when some of the German/Prussian soldiers, that the English had hired, elected to stay in Canada. Germans who were members of the Mennonite religious sect also moved to Canada because their pacifism made them unpopular in the United States.

The 1800s saw German migration, with another influx in the last part of the century and early 1900s. Mennonites from Russia were part of the migration; their ability to farm in the harsh Russian weather helped them succeed in the Canadian Prairie Provinces, with the majority settling in Saskatchewan.

Canada, like the United States, imposed limits on immigration in the 1920s, primarily to limit the number of Eastern European immigrants. That, in turn, limited the number of people trying to get out of Germany with the rise of Hitler and the Nazis.

After World War II, about four hundred thousand Germans immigrated to Canada.

German is one of the largest ancestral groups in Canada, though less identifiable than the French. As in the United States, use of the German language died out after the two world wars and as German immigrants entered the mainstream culture.

Canadian cities with the most people claiming German heritage according to the Canadian census in 2006 are listed as: Toronto, 220,135; Vancouver, 187,410; Winnipeg, 109,355; Kitchener, 93,325; and Montreal, 83,850. Close to half the population in Saskatchewan claims German ancestry.

Prominent Canadians of German heritage include musicians Justin Bieber, k.d. lang, and Randy Bachman, and hockey players Bobby Bauer, and Scott and Rob Niedermayer. Interestingly, Germany began recruiting German-Canadian hockey players in the 1980s. Germany's national hockey team got better, adding the likes of Harold Kreis and Manfred Wolf.

A Brief History of the Germans

If you are an American of European descent, you may have one or more ancestors who came from Germany. No other group is as numerous as the German Americans. Despite two world wars against Germany, the interest of Americans in their German heritage is strong.

The Germanic peoples (or tribes) were known to the ancient Greeks and Romans. But as an entity, the German nation did not exist until 1871—six years after the American Civil War ended.

The wise and scheming Otto von Bismarck (1815–1898), who brought opposing factions together in nationhood, wasn't even born at the time of the American and French revolutions and was only six years old when Napoleon died. The immigration of Germans to America was well under way before and after Bismarck's era.

Germany's background was in the feudal system, which spread through Europe beginning in the eighth century. Under this system, the nobleman held power over his land and its people, up to and including full sovereignty. A sovereign could raise armies, make alliances, and conduct wars. Among other powers, he could collect taxes and tolls. Some people who were immigrating to America paid twenty or more tolls along German rivers.

Out of the feudal system grew the balance-of-power concept. If a candidate for Holy Roman Emperor, together with his relatives and allied friends, was potentially powerful enough to tip the balance, many of the nobility would back a weaker candidate. Secret agreements were common. Breaking agreements was not uncommon. Appeals to the cause of freedom, equality, fraternity, and the rights of man were unheard of.

Weaknesses in the feudal system became obvious. Before it became the practice to bequeath all land to the eldest son, a nobleman's death meant that his domain was divided among all of his sons, leading to a steady increase in the total number of independent land entities. By the middle of the seventeenth century, the land that was to become Germany consisted of more than three hundred separate entities. No wonder there were so many castles. Revolutions in America (1776) and France (1789) shook the world but not the feudal system or the German peasant.

When Napoleon marched through Germany in 1806, many peasants considered it just another change in the managerial class. Continued presence of the French, however, helped stir German nationalistic feelings.

Nationhood would involve centralization of power. Such an increase in power had begun in the seventeenth century in Brandenburg, a northern area that included Berlin. Brandenburg became Brandenburg-Prussia, later known simply as Prussia.

A few facts about the rulers who built this power:

1640–1688 Frederick William the Great Elector, born in 1620, was one of the seven electors whose votes chose the Holy Roman Emperor. These electors were the Duke of Saxony, the Count Palatine of the Rhine, the Margrave of Brandenburg, the king of Bohemia, and the archbishops of Mainz, Cologne, and Trier. Frederick William built a strong and disciplined army, dependent in part on revenues from non-adjacent Cleves and Prussia, and after the 1648 peace of Westphalia, of East Pomerania and the former dioceses of Minden and Halberstadt. As Duke of Prussia, he owed loyalty to the king of Poland but chose armed neutrality after Sweden's King Charles X Gustav overran Poland. Fighting both for and against the Swedes in the 1650s, he won full sovereignty over Prussia. He stripped the estates of their power over taxing and spending and began the establishment of a central government.

1688–1713 Frederick I (born 1657), the son of Frederick William the Great Elector, loaned Emperor Leopold eight thousand Prussian troops and, in return, was proclaimed in 1701 the "King in Prussia," an attempted limitation that failed as he became king of Prussia by general acceptance. In peace treaties, Frederick I won the Swiss canton of Neuchâtel and several enclaves on the lower Rhine. He ran up debts, welcomed French and Dutch Protestants, and founded the Academy of Sciences in Berlin.

1713–1740 Frederick William I (born 1688), son of Frederick I, married Sophie Dorothea of Hanover, daughter of George I of England and sister of George II of England. Frederick William I freed the serfs and made primary education compulsory. Frederick William I also is remembered for his harsh treatment of his son and heir, the future Frederick II the Great. At age 18, the son and his friend and lover, Lt. Hans Hermann von Katte, sought to escape to England but were arrested and tried as army deserters. The future king was forced to witness the beheading of his best friend. Frederick William I also is remembered for what he called his only extravagance—bodyguards who were more than six feet tall. His agents kidnapped one of them in Hesse from a religious group that later founded the Amana Colonies in Iowa. This man served several years before escaping, at risk of execution, by swimming upstream as the search for his body (he was believed drowned) went on downstream. He walked, mostly at night, back to Hesse.

1740–1786 Frederick II the Great (born 1712), grandson of George I of England, decreed an end to religious discrimination, torture in judicial inquiries, press censorship, and the over-six-foot-tall guards. He ordered the laws codified, and he wrote almost daily—in French. With forty thousand men, he overran Empress Maria Theresa's Silesia. With eighty thousand men, he took Prague in 1744. Opposed by Austria, England, Holland, and Sardinia, he fell back but retained Silesia. At age 33, he was called "Frederick the Great." He fought other wars, winning some and losing some, with an army of some one hundred fifty thousand troops. He participated in the 1772 partition of Poland by Prussia, Russia, and Austria, which gave him the lands that had separated East Prussia and Brandenburg. He successfully defied the Holy Roman Empire, beginning its downfall, and enjoyed a brief friendship with Voltaire, the great French author. Also, it was Frederick the Great who forced the peasants to plant potatoes. From the time of Columbus, they had shunned potatoes, convinced that this bounty from the New World was poisonous. They learned otherwise.

1786–1797 Frederick William II (born 1744) was the son of Frederick the Great's brother and came to power after Frederick the Great died childless. In the second and third partitions of Poland, in 1793 and 1795, which wiped Poland off the map, Frederick William II acquired Ansbach, Bayreuth, Danzig (Gdansk), Thorn (Torun), and a large part of central Poland, including Warsaw. Both Mozart and Beethoven dedicated chamber music to Frederick William II.

1797–1840 Frederick William III (born 1770), defeated by Napoleon in 1806, lost all provinces west of the Elbe. But after the 1813 War of Liberation against Napoleon, Prussia acquired Westphalia and traded certain Polish lands for the greater part of Saxony. This gave Prussia responsibilities in both the west and east of Germany, areas that later would be heavily industrialized.

1840–1861 Frederick William IV (born 1795) was an indecisive and relatively ineffective monarch, first opposing and later somewhat favoring the growing demands for a German state.

1861–1888 William I (born 1797), second son of Frederick William

III, became regent in 1858 after his brother suffered a stroke. In 1861, he became King of Prussia. In 1862, William named Otto von Bismarck as prime minister, and Bismarck began guiding Prussia on the path that led to German nationhood. Liberal elements indicated they would accept William I as king of all Germany if he were subject to a powerful legislative body. Bismarck and William I insisted on full power for the monarch. Prussian arms resolved the matter in Bismarck's favor. In the Seven Weeks' War against Austria in 1866, Prussia won control of Hanover, Nassau, Hessen-Kassel, Schleswig-Holstein, and Frankfurt am Main, and excluded Hapsburg-controlled Austria from Germany. In the war of 1870, Germany defeated France. In January 1871, William I, King of Prussia, became German emperor, or kaiser (from Caesar, the family name of the first Roman emperors), at the invitation of the princes of Germany.

1888 Frederick III (born 1831), son of William I, was the first Prussian king to get a college education. He served in three wars—the war against Denmark in 1864, the Seven Weeks' War in 1866, and the 1870 war with France. He was King of Prussia and German kaiser for only ninety-nine days in 1888, when he was voiceless and dying of throat cancer.

1888–1919 William II (born 1859) was the son of Frederick III and Victoria, daughter of Queen Victoria of England. As kaiser, he dismissed von Bismarck in 1890 and set a "new course" in foreign affairs that allied Germany with Austria-Hungary in 1914, leading to World War I. Impetuous and pompous, he lost the support of the military. After the defeat of Germany and the formation of the German Weimar Republic, he lived in exile in the Netherlands until he died in 1941.

1919–1933 The Weimar Republic's weak general assembly faced severe problems after World War I, including crippling inflation and war reparations. Its constitution and experiment in liberal democracy basically ended in 1930, when President Paul von Hindenburg assumed emergency, dictatorial powers. In 1933, Adolf Hitler and the Nazi Party assumed control of government, instituting the Third Reich. The Weimar Republic would continue to exist, on paper, until 1945, and the end of World War II, but 1933 is generally seen as its end.

1933–1945 Adolf Hitler (1889–1945) was an uneducated agitator whose political, managerial, and military inexperience, combined with his vicious hatreds, led to costly miscalculations as he seized power in Germany and started World War II. A few of those mistaken judgments:

- Starting with troops that carried broomsticks, Hitler vowed to build an unbeatable war machine, failing to realize that others could and would respond by building ever bigger war machines.
- Instead of massing his forces, he scattered them—from Norway to Africa, from the Atlantic to the interior of the Soviet Union—waging wars on two fronts at once.
- He failed to comprehend the worldwide revulsion that would result from the gassing of millions of innocent civilians.
- He bombed British cities, ignoring the obvious fact that he was thus inviting retaliatory destruction of the cities and war plants of Germany.
- Where oppressed peoples welcomed his troops with flowers and flags, he took ruthless measures, quickly convincing them that he was not a friend.

In a tragic irony, the defeated and divided Germany became a world showcase of the failures of Communism, on one hand, and the prosperity and freedom of a democracy, on the other. Communism was imposed by Russia in the East, while the West was nurtured and rebuilt by the Allied victors.

Had the world known, in 1918, as much about management of the affairs of nations as was known in 1945, perhaps there would never have been a Hitler and a World War II.

And then, in 1990, as the Soviet Union fell into chaos, the Berlin Wall that separated East and West Germany came down. Germany had reached "the turning point" and again became one country. Germans now celebrate October 3 as German Unity Day.

The country, largely rebuilt after the war, is home to eighty-two million people. Its economy is fourth biggest in the world, and its citizens enjoy one of the highest standards of living in the world. Germany was the first country to offer universal health care. As a republic with free elections and a capital in Berlin, it is among the major political forces in Europe.

Famous German Americans

By Julie McDonald and Mary Sharp

The accomplishments of German Americans are woven so tightly into the fabric of life in the United States that we tend to take them for granted. Among the contributors are:

Eberhard Anheuser and Adolphus Busch In the 1860s, Eberhard Anheuser, a successful German soap manufacturer, teamed with his son-in-law, Adolphus Busch, a wine merchant's son from Mainz, to produce Budweiser beer in St. Louis. The company—which pioneered pasteurization and shipment of beer in refrigerated railroad cars—would become one of the largest in the world. It was sold in 2008 to InBev, a Belgium-Brazilian company, for almost $52 billion. The new company is known as Anheuser-Busch InBev. Other German brewers of renown included Pabst, Schlitz, and Best.

John Jacob Astor He arrived in New York City in 1784 with seven flutes to sell, hoping to open a musical instruments shop. He became a fur trader and, when he died in 1848, he was the richest man in America. He gave away much of his fortune.

Walter Baade (1893–1960) An astronomer who immigrated to the United States in 1931, he discovered major asteroids and made other discoveries related to galaxies, supernovas, and the universe while working in California. A huge telescope in Chile is named after him.

Franz Boas (1858–1942) A cultural anthropologist, he was born in Minden, Germany, but settled in the United States in 1887. He is known for debunking theories on racial "superiority" and for his work with the Kwakiutl Indians in Canada.

William Edward Boeing (1881–1956) William founded the airplane company in Seattle in 1916 that would eventually bear his name and be known throughout the world. He was born in Detroit to a German father who had emigrated from Westphalia in Germany.

George Armstrong Custer This German American distinguished himself in Civil War battles before Indians killed him and 266 of his men at the Battle of Little Bighorn in Montana in 1876. Custer State Park and the town of Custer in western South Dakota honor him.

Dwight D. Eisenhower The thirty-third president descended from a German-Swiss ancestor who arrived in the United States in 1741. Eisenhower distinguished himself as the Supreme Allied Commander in World War II and was president of Columbia University before his successful campaign for the presidency in 1952. The life story of this American leader is memorialized at the Eisenhower Presidential Library in Abilene, Kansas.

Lou Gehrig One of the all-time greats in baseball was born to German immigrants in 1903 in New York City. Gehrig joined the New York Yankees in 1925 and played 2,130 consecutive games—a major league record that stood until Cal Ripken surpassed it in 1995. He had a career batting average of .340, with 493 home runs, including four consecutive ones in the same game in 1932. He died at age 38 of a rare paralysis, amyotrophic lateral sclerosis, which became known as "Lou Gehrig's disease." Another Yankee great, **Babe Ruth,** also was German American.

Manfred George Born in Berlin in 1893, he founded the German-Jewish weekly, *Aufbau,* in New York City. It started as an immigrant newsletter but grew to worldwide circulation. It became known as a forum for those who fled Hitler and for its support of off-Broadway theater.

Michael Heidelberger (1888–1991) Michael is the father of modern immunology. He spent his career at Columbia University. His maternal grandfather was German who immigrated to the United States in the 1840s.

Henry John Heinz The "Pickle King" began packaging food stuffs in Pennsylvania in 1869. The business grew into the H.J. Heinz Company in Pittsburgh in 1888. The company was sold for $23 billion to Berkshire Hathaway in 2013, the largest deal in food business history.

Herbert Hoover The thirtieth U.S. president descended from Andreas Huber, a German-Swiss immigrant who arrived in the United States in 1739. The Hoover birthplace, presidential library, and tomb in West Branch, Iowa, show how Hoover progressed from a tiny house, where he slept in a trundle bed, to a successful business career, and then to the Oval Office.

Abraham Jacobi Born in Westphalia in 1830, the doctor is known as the father of American pediatrics. The city hospital in the Bronx is named for him, and he established the first children's wards at Lenox Hill and Mount Sinai hospitals in New York City.

Henry Kissinger Born in Bavaria in 1923, he became the first German-born U.S. Secretary of State under President Richard Nixon. Kissinger's family immigrated to New York in 1938. He was on the Harvard University faculty and was an adviser to three presidents

(Eisenhower, Kennedy, and Johnson) before being appointed Secretary of State in 1973, the year he won the Nobel Peace Prize.

Ottmar Mergenthaler The inventor of the linotype machine came to the United States in 1872. Linotypes stamped letters and cast them in hot metal; the racks and galleys of letters were used to produce books and newspapers around the world for decades before being replaced by computers in the mid to late twentieth century.

Thomas Nast One of America's most beloved and influential cartoonists, Nast was born in Landau in 1840 and came to the United States when he was 4 years old. He created the image of Santa Claus and the donkey and elephant symbols for the Democratic and Republican parties. His cartoons were critical in the removal of the corrupt Boss Tweed regime in New York City.

Adolph Ochs The longtime owner of the *New York Times* bought the paper, a failing concern, in 1896, and in twenty-five years built it into a widely respected, objective daily. Ochs, who spoke six languages, was born to German-Jewish immigrants in Cincinnati. His only child, Iphigene Bertha Ochs, married Arthur Hays Sulzberger, who became publisher of the *Times* when Ochs died in 1935.

Julius Robert Oppenheimer The brilliant physicist and academic headed the Manhattan Project that developed the atomic bomb at the end of World War II. He was later head of the Institute for Advanced Study at Princeton University. His father emigrated from Germany at the age of 14.

John J. "Black Jack" Pershing The general commanded the American Expeditionary Force in World War I.

Franz Daniel Pastorius Born in Franconia in 1651, he led the first German emigration to the United States in 1683. Arriving with thirteen families on the *Concord,* later known as the *German Mayflower,* he founded Germantown, Pennsylvania, which is now part of Philadelphia.

Johann Georg Rapp The founder of the Harmony Society, among nineteenth-century America's most successful communal groups, Rapp was born in 1757 at Iptingen, Duchy of Württemberg, and became a weaver and vinedresser. He withdrew from the Lutheran state church, believing individuals could independently achieve communion with Christ, and attracted a substantial following by conducting religious gatherings. Resulting conflicts with authorities brought him to the U.S. to find a place to settle free of state interference in religion, and in 1804 founded Harmony, Pennsylvania, north of Pittsburgh, where 900–1,000 ultimately joined him. In

1814, Rapp took the commune to Indiana and built today's New Harmony, then returned it ten years later to establish Economy, now Ambridge, where he died in 1847 and his Harmony Society was dissolved in 1905.

Johann Augustus Roebling The designer of the Brooklyn Bridge died in 1869 after being injured on that job. His son, Washington A. Roebling, oversaw completion of the bridge's construction.

Margarethe Meyer Schurz The wife of Carl Schurz is recognized as the co-founder of kindergarten in the United States. She opened a kindergarten in Watertown, Wisconsin. Another kindergarten was opened in Columbus, Ohio, by another German, **Caroline Louise Frankenberg.**

Carl Schurz An exile from the failed 1848 revolution in Germany, he was nominated for lieutenant governor of Wisconsin before he became an American citizen. (He lost the election.) Schurz was editor of *The Westliche Post* in St. Louis, *The New York Evening Post,* and *The Nation.* He wrote biographies of Abraham Lincoln and Henry Clay. A Union general in the Civil War, he also served as a U.S. senator from Missouri, as Secretary of the Interior under President Rutherford B. Hayes, and as an ambassador to Spain.

Norman "Stormin' Norman" Schwarzkopf Jr. The mediagenic, five-star Army general (and combat veteran) led the American and Allied forces that drove Iraqi troops from Kuwait in 1991 in what became known as the Persian Gulf War.

Charles Proteus Steinmetz Born in Breslau in 1865, he came to the United States in 1889 and became a pioneer inventor for General Electric, where he worked with Thomas Edison. His inventions involved alternating current.

Henry Steinway A German immigrant named Heinrich Engelhard Steinweg—later changed to Henry E. Steinway—founded his famed piano company in New York City in 1853. He and his sons developed the upright piano and prospered.

Levi Strauss This Bavarian immigrant became a supplier to the gold-hungry hordes bound for California in 1850. Strauss, discovering a need for "tough pants" among the prospectors, asked a tailor to make pants from canvas and to rivet the pockets to make them strong enough to hold gold nuggets. The word "jeans" comes from the Italian city, Genoa, where the tough fabric was made. Strauss hated the word. He called his product "overalls."

Henry Villard Born in Germany in 1835, he helped open the

American continent through railroad construction. He was first a journalist and owner of *The Nation* and *The New York Evening Post.* He then raised money for the Northern Pacific Railroad. He was the first president of Edison General Electric, which became the General Electric Company. His philanthropy set an example for the Rockefellers.

John Peter Zenger Born in the Palatinate in 1697, he opened a print shop in New York City in 1726. In 1734, he was jailed for writing and printing articles on nepotism and corruption in government. His wife talked to him through a peephole at the jail and continued his crusade. Andrew Hamilton's successful defense of Zenger established the principle of freedom of the press.

Ferdinand Zeppelin The German count came to the United States as a military observer in the Civil War. He gave his name to the giant dirigibles that appeared in the skies above New York City in 1928. The last dirigible seen outside Germany was the Hindenburg, which exploded and burned at Lakehurst, New Jersey, in 1937.

Quotes From Famous German Americans

"Architecture begins where engineering ends."
Architect Walter Gropius (1883–1969)

"Less is more."
Architect/designer Ludwig Mies van der Rohe (1886–1969)

"When I have a camera in my hand, I know no fear."
Photographer Alfred Eisenstaedt (1898–1995)

"I love mankind. It's people I can't stand."
"Peanuts" cartoonist Charles M. Schulz (1922–2000)

"I think I've discovered the secret of life. You just hang around until you get used to it."
"Peanuts" cartoonist Charles M. Schulz (1922–2000)

"In photography, there is a reality so subtle it becomes more real than reality."
Photographer Alfred Stieglitz (1864–1946)

"Art is the stored honey of the human soul, gathered on wings of misery and travail."
Novelist Theodore Dreiser (1871–1945)

"No good movie is too long, and no bad movie is short enough."
Film critic Roger Ebert (1942–2013)

"If, after I depart this vale, you ever remember me and have thought to please my ghost, forgive some sinner and wink your eye at some homely girl."
Journalist H.L. Mencken (1880–1956)

"A hospital alone shows what war is."
Writer Erich Maria Remarque (1898–1970)

"Ideas are like rabbits. You get a couple and learn how to handle them, and pretty soon you have a dozen."
Novelist John Steinbeck (1902–1968)

"A person's a person, no matter how small."
Dr. Seuss (Theodore Geisel) (1904–1991)

"I want to stand as close to the edge as I can without going over. Out on the edge you see all the kinds of things you can't see from the center."
Novelist Kurt Vonnegut (1922–2007)

"I basically became a cheerleader because I had a very strict mom. That was my way of being a bad girl."
Actress Sandra Bullock (1964–)

"Laughter is much more important than applause. Applause is almost a duty. Laughter is a reward."
Actress Carol Channing (1923–)

"Any girl can look glamorous... just stand there and look stupid."
Actress Doris Day (1924–)

"All your dreams can come true if you have the courage to pursue them."
Entertainer Walt Disney (1901–1966)

"You have to stay in shape. My grandmother, she started walking five miles a day when she was 60. She's 97 today, and we don't know where the hell she is."
Comedian Ellen DeGeneres (1958–)

"I was the editor of the school newspaper and in drama club and choir, so I was not a popular girl in the traditional sense, but I think I was known for being relatively scathing."
Comedian Tina Fey (1970–)

Growing up, I was the plain one. I had no style. I was the tough kid with the comb in the back pocket and the feathered hair."
Actress Cameron Diaz (1972–)

"Always be nice to your children because they are the ones who will choose your rest home."
Entertainer Phyllis Diller (1917–2012)

"America took me into her bosom when there was no longer a country worthy of the name, but in my heart I am German—German in my soul."
Actress Marlene Dietrich (1901–1992)

"I prefer to commit 100 percent to a movie and make fewer films because it takes over your life."
Actress Jodie Foster (1962–)

"I'm six-foot-four, an all-American guy, and handsome and talented as well!"
Actor David Hasselhoff (1952–)

"It was easier to do Shakespeare than a lot of modern movie scripts that are so poorly written."
Actress Jessica Lange (1949–)

"I'm a perfectionist, so I can drive myself mad—and other people, too. At the same time, I think that's one of the reasons I'm successful. Because I really care about what I do."
Actress Michelle Pfeiffer (1958–)

"How can a guy climb trees, say 'Me, Tarzan, You, Jane,' and make a million?"
Actor Johnny Weissmuller (1904–1984)

"I don't see myself as beautiful because I can see a lot of flaws. People have really odd opinions. They tell me I'm skinny as if that's supposed to make me happy."
Actress Angelina Jolie (1975–)

"Between two evils, I always pick the one I never tried before."
Actress Mae West (1893–1980)

"I cannot sing, dance, or act. What else would I be but a talk show host?"
Comedian David Letterman (1947–)

"You fill up my senses/Like a night in the forest/Like the mountains in springtime/Like a walk in the rain/Like a storm in the desert/Like a sleepy blue ocean/You fill up my senses/Come fill me again."
Musician John Denver (born John Deutschendorf) (1943–1997)

"The thing you have to be prepared for is that other people don't always dream your dream."
Singer Linda Ronstadt (1946–)

"A man who has a million dollars is as well off as if he were rich."
Businessman John Jacob Astor (1763–1848)

"In the old days, people used to risk their lives in India or in the Americas in order to bring back products which now seem to us to have been of comically little worth."
Businessman Levi Strauss (1829–1902)

"Being first lady is the hardest unpaid job in the world."
Pat Nixon (1912–1993)

"There are not enough Indians in the world to defeat the Seventh Cavalry."
Gen. George Armstrong Custer (1839–1876)

Growing Up German American

By Bill Eckhardt

The Rev. Bill Eckhardt, a retired Lutheran minister, served for thirty years as pastor at St. Paul Lutheran Chapel, a campus ministry at the University of Iowa in Iowa City. He and his wife, Patricia, now own and operate the historic American House Inn on the Mississippi River in McGregor, Iowa.

German heritage is important to me. I learned many of its characteristics by watching my grandfathers, Ernest Kirchhof of Humboldt County, Iowa, and Frederick Eckhardt Jr. of Boyd, Minnesota.

The two men were quite different from one another, but they also had many similarities. Each was pretty stubborn. I know of few situations where either changed his mind about, well, almost anything. That was both an asset and a liability in hard times, of which they had plenty. Each worked very hard, was frugal, liked to laugh, and respected authority. Each highly valued education, his profession, and his family. Neither they, nor my grandmothers, who shared most of their values, wasted anything, and they severely criticized anyone who did.

Also, they felt a formidable family responsibility, even toward their adult children. For example, three of my dad's four sisters went to college. That was uncommon in the 1920s. My dad and his brothers received a good start in business because of the sacrifices of their generous father.

Frederick Eckhardt Jr. referred to himself as a sausage maker or a butcher. He was that, but he was primarily the owner of a general store.

It was ironic that he, a grocer, had one of the most productive gardens in Boyd, population about 400. Although I rarely saw him work in his garden, neither did I ever see a weed. I probably got up too late in the morning to catch his outside activity.

I did often see him admiring his garden, especially at noontime when he came home for dinner, our largest meal of the day. He loved to walk down the straight rows, occasionally stopping to pick a ripe tomato, pull some carrots, possibly a weed he had missed earlier, or just smile at the beautiful flowers or the purple martins gracefully sweeping away insects overhead.

My grandmother would call to him that the dinner was getting cold, and he'd stomp up the back steps in his large, high-topped, black leather shoes. He'd enter the huge kitchen filled with the aroma of roast beef, chicken, or cooked sausage, potatoes and gravy, and cooked beans or corn or peas. He would sit, say the table prayer, and eat with Grandma and the family. The entire household always ate at the same time, with lively conversation taking place. Then he would usually take a brief nap.

Grandpa Eckhardt also had a small orchard between the community fire station and his huge house. (I visited there years later, and the house was not nearly as large as I'd remember from age eleven.) He liked to walk around the orchard while admiring the apple trees. He might stare critically at an occasional dead branch and resolve to prune it. It was probably gone the next day.

It is likely that his love for the land came from the agricultural traditions of his ancestral home in Germany, where much of the land was owned by absentee nobility. The little that was owned by families was passed from generation to generation, dividing the land among many sons. The parcels became smaller as generations passed, so each square foot was gardened intensively.

Few German yards had grass. Rather, the soil near the houses was filled with plants producing vegetables or flowers. It is not surprising that even in America much of my grandparents' pride came from the beauty of their gardens and how well and economically they could feed their children from those plots.

Both World Wars I and II were hard on my family's German identity. I was told that some of my Eckhardt relatives, especially during the First World War, were occasionally called "kaiser lover" and accused of sympathizing with Germany.

In World War II, my father was drafted at age 36, so I received very little teasing because of my name. On the contrary, I was always so proud to be near my father, especially when he was in uniform.

It was difficult for me to identify the adversary in that war as something or someone German. I always translated the awful things done by the Axis powers to the word "Nazis." I rarely used the word "German" to identify the enemy. This is still true when I reference either war.

My great-grandfather, Frederick Eckhardt Sr., immigrated with his family from Königsberg, Germany, east of the Polish Corridor, to

Rochester, New York, where my grandfather was born. He'd had a long and distinguished career as a Prussian mercenary military officer before being captured and spending several years in a Russian prisoner of war camp in Siberia. He left Germany after he was released because, he said, "All I could see for a future in Prussia was more war." In America, he was a woodworker who did carvings and construction. He spoke seven languages.

I wish I could have met my great-grandfather as he apparently was quite a storyteller. As an entertainer, he often sang, danced, and whistled for buckets of beer. He used his pet monkey to collect coins with a tin cup. Ever since I can remember, I learned how Germany was—and is— the source of so much excellence in music, engineering, science, theology, and many other fields. Most of the people were moral and industrious. I still can't understand how Germany could have spawned so many atrocities and war against America.

But I've drawn two lessons from history: "Be proud of your native land, but not too proud. Let others be proud of their land, too." And: "Chose your leaders very carefully."

My Grandpa Eckhardt's ties to relatives in the Fatherland continued after World War II. He sent generous relief packages to his cousins in Posen, East Germany. Their letters were always censored with bold black horizontal marks, but we were at least able to know they had received the packages and appreciated our help. "Don't bother to enclose any more wooden pencils, though we need them. The Russian censors always open and examine the packages and break pencils into little pieces," the relatives related in one of their letters of thanks.

Recently I rediscovered the accompanying photograph, taken in about 1919, of my grandparents and six of their eleven children posing in their finest clothing. I am sure the photo impressed the rest of the family throughout the States and back in Germany.

The untold story is that they were not as prosperous as the photo might suggest. Louella, the youngest at the time, wore shiny, new black shoes that show plainly in the photo. She confided that her dad would not let her take a step in them. He had to put the shoes back in the box and return them to his store in perfect condition so they could be sold. Shoes were a luxury, not a necessity, especially such nice ones.

My grandparents were quite informed on world events, even by today's standards. They read newspapers, magazines, and listened intently to the radio. My grandpa had a large map of the World War II battle zones on the wall of his meat-cutting room. He'd use it to follow the daily news reports, even though he knew the reports were heavily censored.

My grandparents traveled extensively, taking several trips to Rochester, New York. Wilhelmina Fenski, my grandmother, originally came from Posen, in East Germany. She crossed the Atlantic Ocean twice in a sailboat that was supplemented by steam. The second time she was accompanied only by her uncle. We have the passenger list with her name.

I've given much thought to their influence on me and their view of life as an uncertain, hazardous, but exciting, journey. I think each had an epic personal vision formed with confidence and humility. It made it possible for them to face hardship with such a determination they could pursue their dreams, feel a personal significance in doing so, and enjoy life in the process. I've broken down their approach to life into three parts.

They valued freedom, but valued opportunity even more. They appreciated America for that precious gift so often taken for granted in our country today. They tried to make the most of the opportunities they found here. Their family had known the tyranny of a society where possibilities for advancement were limited. America allowed them to use their personal energy to take care of their families and to expand their horizons. They managed their shortcomings by understanding the importance of the big picture, which included a rich and ennobling past and a confident hope for the future, even in the middle of adversity.

They had hope, based on an ethic of hard work, resiliency, and a fair and generous treatment of others. They passed on that hope to their children. They had faith in a loving and merciful God who had expectations of them. But they strongly felt He also had a plan for them that fit them into this world. "If He can bring me to it, He will bring me through it." Each of my grandparents responded to tragedies in their lives—the loss of several children, severe financial reversals, and health problems, to name a few—with an added faith and resolve. Immediate crises were important—as building blocks and learning tools for the future. They believed the decisions they made were significant, but they did not take themselves so seriously that they couldn't enjoy living.

Top left: Bill Eckhardt, preschooler   Top right with dog: The Rev. Bill Eckhardt
Bottom: Frederick Eckhardt Jr. was born in Rochester, New York, shortly after his parents emi-
grated from Konigsberg, East Germany. Wilhelmina Fenske, whom he would marry, came from
a region known as Posen, east of Berlin, Germany. They considered themselves Prussian. Frederick
and Wilhelmina had eleven children, two of whom, David and Violet, died in infancy and are
buried in Mora, Minnesota. This family portrait shows the remaining children, except for Neva
(whom Wilhelmina was carrying when this photo was taken). The family came to Bancroft,
Iowa, from Rochester, New York, and then moved to Blue Earth and then Boyd, Minnesota,
where this photo was taken and most of the children were born, including Bill's father. The family
members are, in the front row, left to right, Frederick (grandfather of Bill), Louella, and Elsa;
in the back row: Selma, Alfred, Wilfred (the father of Bill), Oscar "Bud," and Wilhelmina.
Frederick was proud of his profession as a mercantile store owner and sausage maker.

—27

What Kind of Welcome in America?

By Eberhard Reichmann

One suitcase and a briefcase—that's all I brought with me when our ship, with lots of emigrants, concluded its eleven-day voyage from Bremerhaven, Germany, to Quebec, Canada, on that misty day November 4, 1953.

A job was waiting for me at Troy Blanket Mills in a little town near Keene, New Hampshire.

When I counted my money after I had purchased my train ticket to Brattleboro, Vermont, I had four Canadian dollars left, enough for a snack on the train and the bus ticket to Keene. From there I would then call my good sponsor, Franklin Fuller Ripley, who was the CEO of the Mill, and he would pick me up. That's the way it was planned.

When the conductor came around I asked him if he knew about the bus connections from Brattleboro to Keene. He said he would check it out. After a while he came back and said, "The last bus leaves at 6 p.m., but we won't get there until 6:20."

Oh my God, if I had to stay overnight at some place I might not even have enough money for the bus. The conductor picked up my befuddled vibrations and said, "Don't worry, let me see what I can do."

"Well, what could he possibly do? Nothing, I was sure," I thought.

An hour later, he stopped again and said, "You'll be okay, my boy."

"What do you mean, me being okay?" I wanted to know.

He said, "The bus is gonna wait for you."

I didn't believe that, I thought he was joking, because buses must be on schedule, they just don't wait, and back in Germany they wouldn't even wait one minute. "Well, how do you know the bus will wait?" I asked.

He said he'd called the bus line. That spelled relief, but not without mixed feelings. For how would the people on the bus react waiting for a German immigrant who might even have been a Nazi?

I thanked the conductor and I was glad it was dark and foggy when I walked over to the bus, expecting a not-so-nice welcome. A man came out of the bus and offered his help with the suitcase. That was nice, but I still expected a thunder of boos inside. Instead, as I stepped inside, I was greeted with a loud *Guten Abend, wie geht's?**

Now, was this a dream or was it real? I found out that an ex-GI who had spent some time in Bavaria had taught his fellow passengers how to welcome a German immigrant. So, even before I got to my New Hampshire "parents," I knew I had made the right choice with America.

Guten Abend, wie geht's? translates into "Good evening, how are you?"

Dr. Eberhard Reichmann

Eberhard Reichmann was born Dec. 8, 1926, in Stuttgart, Germany. After emigrating to the United States in 1953, he attended the University of Cincinnati where he met his future wife, Ruth Backmund, from Bavaria. Ruth and Eberhard were married Dec. 21, 1956.

Eberhard graduated with his doctorate degree in German Studies. He taught at Indiana University Bloomington for 32 years. He retired in 1991, but remained active, producing books, articles, and lectures, particularly in the field of German-American Studies. Dr. Eberhard Reichmann also helped with the production of a Penfield Book's title, *Legends of The Rhine,* by finding wonderful historic illustrations from nineteenth-century books.

In the 1980s, he and his wife, Dr. Ruth Reichmann, researched the German background of Indiana to help preserve that area's heritage.

Eberhard was a multi-talented man. He played several musical instruments, wrote and spoke in English, German, and his native Swabian dialect. He received several honors because of his many accomplishments, including the Federal Cross of Merit First Class, College Teacher of the Year 1990, the Distinguished Service Award, and Hoosier German-American of the Year 2009. He died Oct. 16, 2009.

A German-Russian Girl in North Dakota

By Sister Bernardine Bichler, Order of St. Francis

My parents were Germans from Russia. They came to this country in the early 1900s and settled on a farm in Pierce County, North Dakota. Their Catholic heritage was of utmost importance. When their ancestors fled from Germany to Russia, they built schools and churches.

In North Dakota, there was no church or priest for miles. Every Sunday, the neighbors met at my grandparents' home to pray the Rosary and to read from the Scriptures. After a church was built, a priest came to offer Mass once every two months.

My uncle, a carpenter, built an altar to fit into the corner of our living room. It was painted white with gold trim. On the altar, my mother kept a crucifix, statues of the Blessed Mother and the Sacred Heart of Jesus, two candles, and flowers. Every evening before bedtime, the entire family—parents and ten children—gathered for night prayers before this altar. In summer, I always enjoyed picking wild flowers to decorate the altar, especially for feast days.

All our prayers we learned at our mother's knee. By the time we were old enough to attend catechism classes, we knew all our prayers—in two languages.

My mother was an excellent cook, and she began teaching us to make meals before we reached our teens. She had no recipes. She told me the taste and the texture were her guides. From her I learned to make borscht, a vegetable soup that started with a beef soup bone. It is especially delicious when made with vegetables, including red beets, right out of the garden. The longer one cooks it, the better it tastes. My mother also made all kinds of pasta. I am happy that these ethnic foods are surfacing again and are being enjoyed by the present generation.

Family celebrations were a vital part of our heritage. Weddings lasted three days. The most important part, of course, was the church service. I do not remember a wedding without a dance. Name days of father and mother were also a big treat for us children. All our neighbors and relatives would come together for a big dinner followed by a dance. The music was furnished by family members, relatives, or friends. I believe every German from Russia, young or old, automatically knew how to dance.

Sundays in our home were very special. The meat and dessert for the main meal were prepared on Saturday. During the week, we could not afford any dessert, but on Sunday, there was the best lemon pie! During the summertime, family reunions were special occasions, with outdoor picnics followed by games, usually baseball. All these celebrations strengthened the family, keeping them faithful to family traditions.

My paternal grandmother was a midwife and delivered more than two thousand babies. She delivered nine of the ten children in our family. We were twenty-three miles from the nearest doctor. We had no cars in those days, no paved roads. Our only transportation was horse and buggy. Many years later I happened to meet the doctor who sort of supervised the work of my grandmother. He said, "I never worried when your grandmother took care of the deliveries within that locality." Whenever we saw our grandmother with her black bag, we knew she was on her way to help a woman deliver her baby.

My grandmother was a healer with herbs. Every summer I would see her going to the meadows to pick herbs, and sometimes I went along with her. She had something for a headache, a stomach ache, kidney problems, etc. Now I feel badly that when I began to study nursing I didn't question her about the remedies she used. She grew one plant, chamomile, in her garden. From it, she made tea that was a cure for everything. Even to this day, I love to drink chamomile tea. When one of my brothers fell and received a two-inch gash in his cheek, my parents and grandparents were gone for the week. I was only a teenager, but I remembered grandmother using chamomile tea to wash out wounds. This is exactly what I did, twice a day. I held the wound together with adhesive tape. The wound healed with hardly a scar.

I am deeply grateful to my parents for instilling in me a rich German-Russian heritage, especially the importance of our traditional Catholic religion.

Growing Up in Frankenmuth, Michigan

By Rudolph C. Block

Rudolph C. Block is the former director of curriculum services for the Lutheran Church of the Missouri Synod at St. Louis. He also served as academic dean at Concordia University in River Forest, Illinois.

My great-grandfather Weber was among the first immigrants who settled in Frankenmuth Township in Saginaw County, Michigan.

He and a small group of farmers and craftsmen were sent by Pastor Wilhelm Loehe of Neuendettelsau, Bavaria, to bring the gospel to the Indians. Conversions were few and far between, given that the settlers insisted the Indians first learn German because "God spoke only in German" to them. The colony, however, was quite successful and grew rapidly. The Franconian immigrants built a church and a school. Reading, writing, arithmetic, and religion made up the curriculum, with everything taught in German.

I knew little or no English until I started first grade. Church services in the 1930s were still conducted in Hochdeutsch (Luther's German), and family conversation was all in Bayrisch, a dialect of southern Germany. *Die Fiebel,* a German reading primer, was as important to our early learning as were the Bobbs-Merrill readers.

At our farm home, an important daily ritual involved morning and evening devotions led by my father. He would read a portion of Scripture and a lengthy selection from a devotional book, all in German, of course. We also would often sing a hymn, and we always closed with reciting the Lord's Prayer. And God help any one of us kids—there were four of us—if we should not be listening intently or making some kind of disturbance.

As bedtime neared, my mother took over. She made sure we had done our homework. We learned our first prayers at mother's knee or, should I say, on mother's lap. She went through a short prayer ritual, expecting us to pray along as best we could. As soon as we were able, we recited our evening prayers, and Ma just listened.

My frugal mother also taught me the value of a dollar. Like so many German *Frauen,* my mother was the pivotal member of the family. No decision of any consequence was ever made without her consent and blessing. She controlled the purse strings, keeping a tight rein on any expenditure. She also was generous with family contributions to our church, St. Lorenz. All of our teachers at that time were men. This was neat because they would play ball with us at recess. Families were so supportive of the teacher and his way of doing things that none of us would tattle on another. If a boy received a spanking, and the parents found out about it, he would get twice as hard a spanking at home. Girls in our class wouldn't dream of getting into mischief. They worked overtime trying to please the teacher.

Parents had great love and respect for the teachers of their children. In addition to a cash salary and free housing, the teachers were showered with donations of food and clothing all year. I made frequent trips on Saturdays with my mother to bring the teacher and his family all sorts of produce—a bushel of potatoes, a crate full of carrots, and all types of fruits and vegetables.

My father was a butcher. He spent most of his winter days going from farm to farm all over the township, butchering for relatives, friends, and neighbors. He slaughtered pigs, calves, and cattle, and made the best-tasting summer sausage and every type of sausage imaginable. We had our own smokehouse, so my dad smoked bacon and ham, pork sausage, and summer sausage. The teachers in Frankenmuth, like our pastors, were able to maintain a respectable standard of living, even during the Great Depression. All of the children from the Lutheran families in and around Frankenmuth attended a parochial school. After transferring to the Lutheran central school in uptown Frankenmuth, I was placed in the classroom of the principal, E. F. Rittmueller.

He epitomized the true image of *der Herr Lehrer.* He was extremely strict, and there was no one who didn't fear him. Yet he was also fair, had a good sense of humor, was generous with deserved praise, and seemed to be an absolute authority on just about everything. Being selected by him to serve on the school's safety patrol squad was a coveted honor. Serving as lieutenant of the squad (with the captain, who was my best friend) during eighth grade was about as neat as being selected to play the Angel Gabriel in the all-school Christmas pageant. Needless to say, whatever doubts remained about my future were wiped out. I wanted to be a teacher just like Mr. Rittmueller.

At our graduation, where I was the class speaker, my parents beamed with pride and joy as I publicly announced my decision to study for the teaching ministry. It was a tradition that religiously devout parents with more than one son would dedicate one of them for service to the Lord as a pastor or teacher. St. Lorenz of Frankenmuth contributed well over 500 of its sons (and recently daughters as well) to the ministry in its first 125 years.

My generation was the last to receive a bilingual education in Frankenmuth. My class also was the last to be confirmed in German. We had German readers that progressed from grade to grade parallel to the readers in English.

As I look back now with fond and happy memories, I am saddened by what World War II did to the people of Frankenmuth. Five years after my graduation, German had been eliminated as a required part of the curriculum. It was then taught only as a foreign language. That did not stop the farm kids from using Bayrisch.

Although Martin Luther championed general education, the general attitude of the German farm families in Frankenmuth was that higher education was not to be "wasted on girls." Daughters were expected to learn how to clean, bake, and sew, as well as help with the chores on the farm. That would make them into fit wives for farm boys who had become men and were ready to get married. The Franconians saw the necessity of a college education, however, and the importance of higher education spread beyond the professions.

Among my earliest childhood memories is how we spent our Sundays. To begin with, we never failed to go to church on Sunday morning. Then came a fine noon meal, usually a great chicken dinner with all the trimmings. Next came an afternoon visit to the home of one of our many relatives. While our folks visited, we children played elsewhere in the big house or outside with our many cousins. It was a form of the extended family.

A young couple contemplating marriage wouldn't dream of eloping or having a justice of the peace perform the ceremony. Marriage vows were spoken in church, with one of the pastors performing the ceremony. Special friends of the family would be selected to supervise the gathering of all the delicious homemade bread, pies, and cakes. The main course would generally be veal, chicken, or beef, with mashed potatoes and gravy, and home-grown vegetables.

The one fly in the ointment was having to do chores between the wedding ceremony and the dinner and reception later. The cows needed to be milked twice a day, seven days a week. The wedding I recall most vividly was that of my brother, who was five years my senior. Not only was I his best man, but I did not have to go home to do the chores. The wedding reception was quite typical of Frankenmuth weddings in the middle of the twentieth century.

After the big dinner in the church grove, a lengthy program would be presented honoring the bride and groom and also embarrassing them a bit by digging out, or manufacturing, stories that would thoroughly amuse the gathered celebrants. The introduction of various family members and friends by the master of ceremonies would be interspersed with jokes and stories meant to amuse. At the appreciation hour, the best man would lead the assembly with a loud and musical *Sie leben hoch* (They live high!). Beer and wine flowed freely, and dancing would start just as soon as the pastor, or pastors, had found a convenient time to say goodbye to the happy couple.

No real wedding celebration was complete without a shivaree. Friends of the groom who were not invited to the wedding would gather in a group of six to a dozen to interrupt the celebration by making a racket that would wake the dead. They clanged heavy hammers on various size heavy metal discs, starting and ending each round with a stick of dynamite. The object was to pretend to steal the bride or at least interrupt the festivities. After three or four rounds of this noise-making, the groom would go out and dicker with them, offering them a keg of beer and some money to leave in peace.

Around midnight, the bride would cut the first piece of a huge wedding cake and literally stuff it into the bridegroom's mouth. Each guest would then receive a piece of cake along with coffee, tea, or soda. Then several husky members of the bridal party would hoist the bride and groom, seated on chairs tied together with crepe paper, high into the air—all to the rousing cheers of three more *Sie leben hoch!*

Growing up German in America was quite an experience for those of us lucky enough to be born in Frankenmuth.

Memories From a St. Louis Childhood

By Paul L. Maier

An educator, religious writer, and novelist, Paul L. Maier, born May 31, 1930, was the Russell H. Seibert Professor of Ancient History at Western Michigan University. Maier retired in the spring of 2011.

Although my father's radio broadcasting career was an American success story—he was Walter A. Maier, founder of *The Lutheran Hour*—his roots were totally Teutonic.

A son of German immigrants who settled in Boston, he married Hulda A. Eickhoff of Indianapolis in 1924, a union of total German ethnicity, as the names suggest. Both, however, spoke English without a trace of an accent—unlike their parents.

But since they had been raised in families where German was spoken before English, they attempted the same with their own children, my brother, Walter Junior, and me.

Brother Walt carried on with the German longer than I did, but his bilingualism was quickly curtailed the first time he played with the neighbor boys and asked them to throw him a ball by saying, *"Gib mir den ball!"*

"So who's that foreigner?" they shouted derisively.

German was shunted aside after that, except in family devotions where the Lord's Prayer was uttered about half the time in the mode, *"Vater unser...."* Our bedtime prayers, too, continued in German, a string of brief hymn verses and Bible passages—the same series we all recited together at Father's bedside as he lay dying in January 1950.

By the 1930s, both parochial and Sunday school instruction were in English.

One of the earliest recollections of my childhood days was a conversation I had with my mother—in German. When I was a toddler, she used to take me sightseeing to churches near our home in St. Louis County. But one day she varied the routine by visiting a synagogue. I looked around inside and asked, *"Aber wo ist der liebe Heiland?"* ("Where is the dear Savior Jesus?") When mother explained that worship there did not involve Christ, I replied, *"Komm, lasst uns gehen."* ("Come, let's go.")

In the spring of 1935, the Walter A. Maier family served as patrons of German art for the city of St. Louis. The famed 700-year-old Dredner Kreuzchor—the Boys Choir of Holy Cross College of Dresden, Germany—was planning its first American tour after a debut at the Metropolitan Opera House in New York City. Father and Mother, with the help of interested friends, sponsored the St. Louis appearance at a full Municipal Opera House, with prolonged ovations and enthusiastic reviews.

We housed two of the choristers overnight at our home on the grounds of Concordia Seminary in St. Louis. En route to the concert, my brother tried to restore the German *Sprachgefühl* we were both losing by asking them, *"Sprechen sie Deutsch?"*

"Ah, … ja natürlich!" one responded, in disdain.

So much for small talk in a foreign language! Mother also hosted German-speaking parties at our home, some of which were attended by the German consul and his wife, until the nefarious shadow of Adolf Hitler put an end to all that in the late 1930s.

Every Christmas, the Maier family celebration began with Father at the piano playing (by ear) the German Yuletide folksong, *"Kling, Glöckchen, Kling-a-ling-a-ling"* ("Ring, Little Bell"). The rest of the family sang the lyrics lustily while clanging bells and chimes of every description, as we all marched in festive procession through the house during endless choruses.

Grandmother Maier, whom we called "Grossie" (for *Grossmutter*), often visited us at Christmastime. Born in picturesque Rothenburg in southern Germany, she never lost her German accent. With her, "faith" and "fate" received the same pronunciation. Before Christmas, Grossie filled the air with the fragrance of cookies baked from wondrous European recipes. We were convinced that her *Prügelkrapfen* would be the official cookie in heaven.

Whenever the Maier family embarked on a vacation, Father would lead us in prayer for a safe journey. The invocation always began, *"Unsern Ausgang segne Gott, unsern Eingang gleichermassen…"* ("May God bless our leaving and our coming as well"). As we were driving, however, if an automobile accident seemed imminent, Mother would cry out, *"Gott behütte uns!"* ("God protect us!") We had not a few accidents on those narrow, twisting roads of the 1930s, and the younger Maiers grew to detest Mother's three-word shout because it always seemed to herald disaster.

Mother's three sisters in Indianapolis were not our aunts, but *"die Tanten,"* and whenever they visited us at our summer home along Lake Ontario, morning table devotions often began with what Walt and I (now thoroughly Anglicized) irreverently called "Fang Song"—*"Fang dein Werk mit Jesu an"* ("With the Lord begin thy task"). At day's end, Father and Mother often stood arm-in-arm along the lakeshore and serenaded the setting sun with the song, *"Seh, wie die Sonne dort sinket."*

Although my mother was born and raised in Indiana, speaking and writing English perfectly, the German confirmation instruction she received and the German hymns she learned remained with her indelibly throughout life, especially toward its close. During the months before she passed away in 1986—on her ninety-sixth birthday—she would recite endless verse of German hymns from memory, finding extraordinary inspiration and comfort in them.

Christianity and music, then, served as the most reliable conduits for German culture in our family. I doubt that our experience is unique.

Dancing Through Life

By Karin Gottier

As long as I can remember, folk dance has captured my imagination. On warm summer evenings, I would stand by the fence in the corner of our garden in Germany and watch as the "big" boys and girls left to go folk dancing. Because they always came back singing and laughing, I decided that as soon as I was old enough, I would go folk dancing a lot.

When I was six years old, I was a flower girl at a rural wedding in East Prussia. After a long train ride, we traveled by horse and wagon through dark pine forests to the farm where the wedding was to be held. It was 1943.

The following evening was *Polterabend:* Neighbors came to break dishes and glasses in front of the bride's door. She had to sweep away the shards and invite people in for coffee and cake and stronger refreshments.

The next morning, the wedding day, the doors of the farmhouse were wreathed in pine garlands, and the draft oxen's horns were decorated with paper flowers and ribbons. The threshing floor was cleared, and large boards were placed over sawhorses, then covered with linen bed sheets to serve as banquet tables. The posts of the barn also were garlanded, and a space was set aside for the musicians. There was coming and going all day as neighbors brought piles of cakes and helped with the cooking.

After the ceremony, which was performed by a woman pastor (the first German woman minister was ordained in 1932), the procession was waylaid by the village children, who had stretched a green rope across the street. The bridegroom was obliged to "buy" our passage by tossing coins and candy into the crowd of children.

Then, after a long and ample meal, several guests and children presented small sketches and poems appropriate to the occasion. Later there was dancing. People danced the usual dances that were popular in the 1940s—fox trot, two-step, with a waltz or a polka thrown in. As the party went on, older people began to do dances with figures, dances that looked like much more fun than what had been danced earlier. They also sang as they danced. For me, it was a revelation: "So that is what folk dance looks like!" Later, the women who had cooked all day came out of the kitchen and danced while holding out their aprons, into which the guests tossed small coins.

We children were supposed to sleep under the roof in a very small room with sloping sides that was reached only by a very precarious structure, more ladder than stairs. That night I woke with a start to discover that the bride was hiding among us. The married women were looking for her, intent on tearing her veil at midnight, but they had to catch her first. Of course, they found her and, with much clamor, took her back to the party.

These were the war years. When the war finally ended, on a radiantly beautiful May day with clear blue skies, birds singing, flowers blooming, and bees buzzing, the entire manmade world was a smoking heap of rubble. Burned war equipment, dead soldiers of both armies, burning and smoking houses, and downed power lines were everywhere. The following day my mom sent me on an errand into the village, which was on the outskirts of greater Berlin. The path I had to take cut through a field where the last battle had been waged. Without looking left or right, in order to not see the dead soldiers, I stared straight ahead and ran as fast as I could.

Coming through the center of the village on my way home, I saw a Russian army truck parked in the shade of a large chestnut tree along the street. One soldier sat on the hood playing his accordion, a second one stood clapping in rhythm, and the third danced one of those vigorous male dances so typical of Russians. I looked around to see for whom they were performing, and seeing no one, I realized they were playing and dancing for their own enjoyment. As I watched, I began to wonder why we humans all dance so differently. Looking back, I am convinced that this was one of the precious moments that set me on my life's path.

As May turned into June, a notice was posted in town that all children were to report to school. When we gathered, those of us who had gone to school there before were outnumbered by strange faces and dialects. The school had lost its windows and roof shingles, all of its doors, and most of its desks. A young man, himself barely out of the teens, was to bring order into this chaos. He resorted to a quick method of sorting us out: "How old are you? What can you read? Read this paragraph, okay, third grade. Next!"

I found myself in third grade together with sixty other children, some of whose German was so strange that we could hardly talk to each other. They were children who'd had to leave their homes in East and West Prussia, Silesia, Slovakia, Hungary, and elsewhere. Many didn't know where their parents were. Others had become orphans on their wintertime trek across Northern Europe, ending up in Berlin at war's end.

None of us had much clothing. Arms and legs stuck out too far from sleeves and pant legs. Shoes had their toe caps cut out to allow for growth, or we wore sandals made of old rubber tires. But we natives had homes and a place where we belonged. These other children were without even that. This, then, was the makeup of the class that our young teacher was supposed to teach. We had no paper and no books. Chalk was a precious commodity that the teacher carefully carried around with her in an empty bandage box. But we coped valiantly, and soon winter approached.

By now it had become apparent to the occupation forces that it would be extremely difficult to supply Berlin with food and fuel during the winter. Consequently, the British military authorities organized a program called *Aktion Storch* (Action Stork). The objective was to remove as many children as possible from Berlin and to ship them to the British zone, an area of Germany that had seen little bombing or fighting. We left by train at 5 a.m. on a gray, foggy November 1. After hours of traveling through flat countryside, we transferred to army trucks and spent the night at a British military camp after being deloused by huge syringes that sprayed yellow powder down our necks and sleeves. We spent the night on army cots in tents and then got back in the trucks for more travel. I had never been so far away from home in all of my nine years. I had no idea where we were.

Still, it was a grand adventure. The land continued to become flatter. Huge, brick and straw-thatched houses seemed to duck into the landscape or huddle in a cluster of old trees. Fat cows were grazing everywhere. It seems that we had driven for hours in a cold drizzle when suddenly the truck made a sharp turn, came to a stop, and there—in front of me—was the vast, gray expanse of the Atlantic Ocean.

I had heard about oceans, especially the Baltic, from my father who came from there. But I was unprepared for such a sudden confrontation with this overwhelming endlessness. My immediate reaction was to cover my face with both hands and to duck. When nothing happened, I cautiously moved my fingers, one at a time, and peeked out. We were at a pier, so we surely must have arrived, since there was nowhere else to go.

Soon we were bundled into a resort steamer that served as a ferry and headed out to sea. Most of us got caught up in the excitement and didn't notice that the sea was running high with large, white-foam crests. While our adult companions were slowly turning green below deck, we were roaming around topside, cheering the seagulls that followed the steamer.

After a relatively short time, the ship docked, and we children huddled together in the center of the cobblestone harbor. The mayor, our welcoming committee, informed us that we were on the island of Norderney, off the north coast of Germany, and that there was no more room for refugees. But since we were there, he said, he would have to put us up somehow. While he made his speech, I crept away from the group and hid behind two young men who had happened to be watching.

In my best Berlin slang, I said, "I ain't goin' where they don't want me." The young men turned around and smiled, and one said, "What have we here? A genuine Berlin big mouth, eh?"

Ultimately, some of us were settled in a Lutheran Children's Home for the night. The Sisters were totally unprepared for a sudden invasion of such a large group in the middle of winter. There was no food, no heat, and no light, but they rose to the occasion. Early the next morning, I crept out of the garden and followed the sound of the surf, which led me to the beach at low tide. What a discovery! There was a whole world in those tide pools on the breakwater: starfish, shells, and assorted creepy-crawlies that I promptly gathered into my handkerchief.

When I found my way back to the home with my treasures, a Sister told me of a family with a toddler who would like a girl to look after and play with her. She told me to meet them, and we liked each other immediately. So I became part of a family that consisted of parents, several young adult sons, a daughter-in-law, and a baby.

While the young men were seafaring, the rest of the family operated a store that was in the front of the house. The house, like all houses on the island, featured a large, glassed-in veranda and rooms for summer guests.

The first evening I sat in awe of the large, blue-and-white tiled kitchen and marveled at the sausages and bacon sides threaded on rods along the ceiling. While the housemother was busy frying flounders for supper, the door opened, and two young men walked in. We looked at each other and laughed. They were the same young men I'd hidden behind at the harbor the day before. Now I really felt at home.

We children from Berlin went to school in the afternoon—double shift with the local children—and again the teacher had to cope with sixty students of various levels, without any educational materials.

As time went on, I learned to understand the Low-German dialect and to appreciate the 4 o'clock tea time. I explored the town, roamed the dunes and the beaches, and fell totally in love with the island and its culture, especially when I discovered the people there who wore native dress and folk-danced.

Every week, a group of young men and women wearing their folk costumes came to the house to pick up one of the sons. They were all members of the local "Homeland Guild" that met to cultivate their songs, dances, and traditions. They went folk dancing!

Despite all my pleading to go along and watch, I was told once again that I wasn't old enough. By now, I was more determined than ever to become a folk dancer. A slightly older neighbor girl, who knew some of the local dances, finally took me down to the beach at low tide and showed me some simple dances that we danced over and over again.

In due time, it became spring. On May 1, we all boarded the white steamer again, this time in bright sunshine, to return to Berlin. As the steamer pulled away, there were tears on both sides of the dock because we had become fond of our foster families and they had become fond of us. Some of the Action Stork children stayed in touch with their foster parents and siblings for years.

A Red Cross train took us back to Berlin where the lilacs were blooming, and a place in the ballet school was waiting for me. That summer, my father died. After that, my mother and I got along as best we could. I was the only child of their marriage. Then came the blockade of Berlin with its food shortages and power and fuel rationing. These were very cold and very hungry days. The whole world seemed gray, and the adults were hopeless and discouraged.

Because the ballet school was affiliated with an operetta theater, I had the opportunity to participate in some of their productions and was very wrapped up in ballet. One day a classmate told me there was folk dancing in our gym after school. But by now I had become a snob: "Folk dancing is for people who can't dance any better."

Nevertheless, I went to the dance after school. It was absolute, passionate, unconditional love at first step. This was what I had been looking for all my life. Everything else fell by the wayside while I went folk dancing and, because the dances were organized by the Tourist Club of Nature Friends, also hiking and youth hosteling.

Finally, I was old enough to go folk dancing! By now, I was fifteen, and my mother had become very ill. Because there were no other relatives, and all her sisters and brothers were in America, they invited me to come and live with them. I spent the first six years in Connecticut pining for folk dancing and for my friends at home. There was an all-girl folk dance group in high school with a repertoire of exactly three dances, but it wasn't the same. In order to not forget the dances from home, I went alone into the backyard to dance, without music, each part as it came up in the dance.

After graduating from high school, I went to work at a department store while going to college in the evening. After being a buyer for a number of years, I became the youth coordinator assigned to develop merchandising programs for teenagers. What an opportunity to start an informal folk dance group with the store's Teen Board!

One day, while in New York City on business, I happened to walk past a red door with big letters announcing "FOLK DANCE HOUSE." I opened the door, walked in, and was home. Folk Dance House, under the direction of Michael and Maryanne Herman, also directed a folk dance camp in Maine dedicated to the dance and folklore of all nations. The vacation that I spent there was the beginning of a new direction in my life. After marriage and a child, I did graduate work in German Studies. With encouragement from the Hermans, I began to teach German folk dance and folklore.

It is now more than seventy years since I came to America. Yet each time I give a workshop in the dances and folk culture of the different German regions, my homeland is here with me through its dances and traditions. When I returned to Germany to dance and research, it felt as though I had never left. Dance has been the bridge between my old homeland and my new home.

A Long, Extraordinary Journey

By Mary Sharp

Brigitte as *a teenager*

Brigitte Müller was 12 years old, living in a Berlin suburb and having breakfast, when she heard on the radio that German troops had rolled into Poland. It was September 1, 1939.

She delivered the news to her father, who was already at work in the family's attached *Drogerie* (drugstore). She remembers that her father a veteran of World War I, was shocked by the news. He had hoped for a peaceful settlement.

Brigitte—now Brigitte Meyer-Jenniges—would marry an American G.I. after World War II. She moved to Cedar Rapids, Iowa, in 1949 and would have five children with that soldier, Willard "Bill" Meyer. She became a U.S. citizen in 1953.

The war years remain vivid in her memory. At the time, she recorded her experiences in a diary, but she doesn't need to look up the dates and the details. She remembers them, and she regularly shares them with schoolchildren and her extended family. She also came through the war's harrowing years with a thought or two on life. "It's the same in every country," she says. "The ordinary people are kind and good, with some good ones and some bad ones thrown in. ... No war solves any problems."

Brigitte's father and mother, Franz and Gertrude Müller, operated two drugstores in the Berlin suburbs. She had one sister and then two half-brothers after her parents divorced. She was good at school and went on to high school during the war. She didn't join the Hitler Youth, saying she went to a meeting once and "didn't like it." Her schooling, she adds, was free of politics.

After Allied air raids began in Berlin in August 1943, she voluntarily evacuated with some of her classmates to Chrudim, Czechoslovakia. The students and teachers stayed in a hotel, sharing the school building on alternate weeks with Czech students. The class even managed a memorable field trip to Prague in the spring of 1944.

Brigitte passed her final exams and graduated early, in November

1944. She visited her parents for a week before reporting for mandatory six-month national service in Czechoslovakia. She was then "drafted" to help at a military hospital—actually a converted police barracks—in Mladá Boleslav, Czechoslovakia. She arrived there on March 22, 1945.

It was an eye-opening experience for the naïve seventeen-year old. Soldiers were brought to the hospital straight from the Russian front. She cleaned and fetched water, "doing all the little things that were necessary. I'd always gone to girls' schools. How I stood it, I don't know. Once, I even had to do things in the operating room." The hospital ran out of medicine and supplies and began wrapping wounds in something like crepe paper. The dressings were changed infrequently, with disinfectant injected under the paper.

"People cannot imagine what war can be like," Brigitte says as she recalls by name some of the men she cared for more than sixty-five years ago.

On April 19, 1945, the Russian front was only forty-five miles from the hospital. The young helpers who'd been drafted were told they could leave and go home, if they could get there. By then, much of Germany was controlled by Allied troops, so many of the young helpers had nowhere to go. But Brigitte wanted to try to either get home to Berlin or to Lychen, sixty-five miles north of Berlin, where her maternal grandparents lived. She left the hospital the next day with an officer—a lieutenant named Joe (more about him later)—who needed to rejoin his unit in Berlin. They were able to catch two trains, until they reached the outskirts of Dresden, which had been heavily damaged in bombing.

Then they had to start walking, even though Joe was still using a cane. Joe told her she'd have to leave her suitcase behind. She protested: "'All I have is in that suitcase.' And so I went to a house across the road and knocked on the door. 'Could you keep this for me until I can come back sometime?' They said yes." (She would never see that suitcase again.) Brigitte and Joe walked for nine days toward Berlin. They slept in barns and ate when they could. "I don't know how we got through it all," she says. "We didn't have ration cards with us. People were good to us." Joe left to join another unit—"he had to, or he would have been shot as a deserter"—leaving the seventeen-year old on her own.

It was impossible to enter Berlin, which was surrounded by Russian forces. Lychen was on the front line. She ended up on a road near Plau, Mecklenburg, where a wood-burning cattle truck stopped so the driver could chop more wood. He agreed to give her and another girl a ride.

Brigitte remembers it snowed that night—April 30, unusual for Germany—and that she and the other girl huddled together for warmth against the truck's cab. The ride ended at the marketplace in Schwerin, Mecklenburg, still about a hundred miles west of Lychen. Brigitte remembered the address of a former classmate who lived in Schwerin. She went there on May 1, and "they took me in."

American troops took the city on May 2. The war in Europe ended May 8. Bridgette did not know if her family was alive. She hadn't heard from them in more than four months—there was no postal service, no telephone service.

Determined to find out their fate, Brigitte saw a posting from a woman and her two children who wanted to return to Lychen. Russian troops were in control of that city and had just taken over Mecklenburg from the Americans (as agreed by the Allies at the Yalta Conference).

A man, who somehow had access to diesel fuel, was driving a tractor to Lychen, pulling a hay wagon behind. Brigitte and the woman laid a carpet over the wagon as a makeshift roof. At night, the woman had Brigitte lie under the wagon's axle, with the woman's young sons on each side of her. The woman took off their shoes, so Russian soldiers wouldn't know a young girl was sleeping there.

After three days, the group safely arrived in Lychen—"I don't know how to find the town's center"—because it had been destroyed by fire.

Brigitte immediately saw a woman who had once worked for her grandmother. She called out, "Erika—are they still alive?"

"Oh, yeah, they are."

Heartened by that news, Brigitte walked around the lake to her grandparents' home. She remembers her grandparents sitting in their "beautiful yard," cleaning green beans as she walked into view.

"They didn't trust their eyes," she says.

After the greetings, and the relief, she learned that her mother, sister, and half-brother, who'd been staying there, had just left for Berlin after learning their home would be confiscated if they didn't return. "I knew I had to go there," Brigitte says. Her grandmother wanted her to go, too, knowing "terrible things were happening every night" in Lychen during the occupation.

Once more, the resourceful Brigitte found a man, the father of one of her friends, who had come to Lychen from Berlin to see if his mother was still alive. He said Brigitte could travel with him. Her grandparents dug out the stroller her little brother had once used. They tied extra clothing and a feather tick to the stroller. Brigitte and the man left Lychen at 5 a.m. July 17. The man wisely chose to stay on the road instead of cutting through the woods where soldiers stopped refugees.

After walking about eight miles, Brigitte and the man made it to a railway station where they were lucky enough to find an operating steam train pulling out of the station, taking a Russian general to the Potsdam peace conference. They literally jumped aboard one of the freight cars attached to the train. The stroller made it, too. They also were smart enough to get off the train before it reached the center of Berlin, where many refugees were, again, relieved of their possessions.

Brigitte worked her way toward her mother's home, walking and riding what was left of the subway system, only to find the home abandoned. "It hadn't been bombed. My room was on the third floor of our house. The key was in the lock, which was unusual. Everything was in good shape, clean and orderly, just like my mom always insisted it to be. Flowers were on the table. But nobody was around."

Looking out the window, she saw an American soldier and, remembering some of her school-day English, asked him where everyone was. In a gruff voice, he asked her what she was doing there. After all the miles, privations, and worry, she finally—for the first time—cried.

"This was our house," she said.

The soldier, feeling sorry for her, gave her a roll of Life Savers® and said the house had been confiscated for U.S. officers' quarters. Although her mother had left no note about where she'd moved, a neighbor, who'd also been moved, had left a note with a new address. After further delays and runarounds, Brigitte finally found the neighbor, who said her mother had relocated to another suburb of Berlin.

Brigitte knew the way and again began walking. But when she came to a canal she had to cross, she found the bridge destroyed. What to do? An old man warned her she needed to get inside quickly since it was getting dark and the Allied curfew was strictly enforced. He then showed her where Russian soldiers had laid two wide planks across the canal. She crept across, pulling the stroller, as water splashed through the planks.

"I took my life in my own hands." Just before curfew, she found the house where she hoped her mother was staying. She knocked on the door. The door opened, and there was her mom.

"I made it," she said. Though they were happy to see each other, her mother, who was living with her in-laws, told her there wasn't room for another person. Brigitte would have to live with her father. So once more, Brigitte began walking. But this time, it took only a little while until she walked into her father's drugstore. She found him looking for items in the attic.

Brigitte said, "Hi, Dad."

Her journey from Czechoslovakia to Berlin had taken three-and-a-half months. "My grandmother raised us to be Christians. I know she prayed for us all the time," Brigitte says. "I saw terrible, sad things in getting to my house. I know God took care of me all of that time."

Brigitte wanted to go to college but felt she needed to help her family. She completed a short course for English interpreters. She was hired by the U.S. occupation forces and met her husband during that job. She went through the Berlin air lift, while her husband-to-be was transferred to Heidelberg in southern Germany. They wanted to marry, but the military would not allow U.S. Army soldiers to marry a German citizen until four weeks before returning to the United States. They finally married on May 14, 1949. Brigitte, with one child in hand and pregnant with her second child, arrived in Cedar Rapids, her husband's home town, on September 1, 1949. Their son was born September 23.

Willard (Bill) Meyer and Brigitte Müller, 1947

Brigitte says she and Bill had a normal, happy life in Cedar Rapids, working and raising their children, until Bill, one day after work, died of a sudden heart attack, at age 47, in February 1975. For the next nine years, she says, "I struggled to take care of all the things that had to be taken care of. I worked late hours and was able to pay off the mortgage on our house."

But the story's not done. After her husband's death, Brigitte was at coffee with some German women friends. One of them was from Cologne, where, Brigitte remembered, that young lieutenant, Joe Jenniges, had lived before they took their nine-day walk at the end of the war. It got her to thinking.

She found Joe's phone number. She called. It had been thirty-eight years since they'd seen or talked to each other. Joe had married and had five children but was separated at the time. He visited Brigitte in 1984. They kept in touch.

Mary Sharp photos

Brigitte Meyer-Jenniges, age 86   *Joe Jenniges, age 90*

Joe and Brigitte married in 1988 and now live in a comfortable home in Marion, Iowa. Brigitte has assembled her family's history in twelve bound notebooks. It's for the kids and grandkids "so they can know about their German ancestors. I hope they treasure it."

From Germany to Iowa

By Mary Sharp

Christoph Trappe

Christoph Trappe was sixteen years old when he left Düsseldorf, Germany, in 1995 and moved half a world away to go to high school in Iowa City, Iowa. He's now 35, a U.S. citizen, and among the top young professionals in Cedar Rapids, Iowa.

When Christoph arrived in the United States, he was a foreign exchange student at Iowa City West High School, playing football there for two years. He was recruited to play football at the University of Iowa, where he was a scholarship player for four years, graduating with a degree in journalism in 2001.

Christoph worked for daily newspapers in Muscatine, Iowa City, and Cedar Rapids, Iowa, and for a video training company before becoming vice president of communications and innovation for United Way of East Central Iowa in Cedar Rapids. He is now senior client relationship manager for MedTouch, a web marketing company for medical businesses and services.

Christoph married Rachel Ott, and they have two daughters, Sophie and Ellie. He became a U.S. citizen in 2008. Which has to count as quite a story in anyone's book.

"You set a goal and kind of go for it," Christoph says.

Christoph is a big guy and started getting interested in American football when he was thirteen and playing club sports in Germany, where he met some U.S. football players, including some former University of Iowa Hawkeyes. Then he saw Joe Montana and the 49ers play a pre-season NFL game in Berlin.

"I was hooked," he says.

While lifting weights at *Rheinstadion* (Rhine Stadium), he became interested in how one man always seemed to be telling stories. He found out the man was a journalist and thought that might be something he'd like to do, too.

So his thinking became two-pronged. If he wanted to play football, he needed to move to the United States. If he went to the United States, he needed to learn English.

There were two ways to do that, his teacher in Duisburg told him: Study English vocabulary really hard or move to the United States.

So moving to the United States made sense, and Christoph began investigating how to become a foreign exchange student.

It took a while, but he remembers the day he received the phone call telling him that Tony and Chris Forcucci in Iowa City would be his host family. At that exact moment, he says, he was wearing an Iowa Hawkeyes' shirt given to him by former Hawkeye linebacker John Hartlieb.

The Forcuccis told Christoph they lived just down the street from Kinnick Stadium, where the Hawkeyes play their home games.

It took a year to make all the arrangements. Christoph went through an orientation where the U.S.-bound students were encouraged to smile a lot—"to show your teeth"—in a country where most people are "very friendly."

Was it hard to make the decision to leave Germany and live abroad?

"Not really," Christoph says. "I would have kicked myself all my life had I not taken the opportunity.

"When I put on that (Hawkeye) uniform and went on the field, I thought, 'I'm on a Division I football team.' How does that not outrank being at home, joining the military for two years, and then trying to get back in that groove? Here, I might make it to the NFL, I might not. But, at the very least, I'm going to get an education. So there really wasn't anything negative that you could foresee.

"These are the things you have to think about—what's important in your life? What kind of advice would you give your best friend if he had to make the same decision?" That said, the path to U.S. citizenship was "a lot of work." He adds, "It takes a long time, it's complicated, and it's expensive."

But, again, it was a clear-cut choice.

"You live here. This is where your life is. Why wouldn't you do it?"

Only in America

By Anneliese Heider Tisdale

Kadlec Photography
Anneliese Heider Tisdale

Editor's Note: This is a chapter from Anneliese Heider Tisdale's memoir, *Christmas Trees Lit the Sky.* The book tells of her childhood in Munich, Germany, during World War II. This excerpt relates her departure from Germany, on her way to a new life in America.

Friday, June 13, 1947. Our plane has just taken off from Frankfurt Airport and is now gaining altitude. In the seat next to me is my cousin Mariele. We are both German war brides.

As I look down, the bombed-out ruins of the city stare back at me like the empty eye sockets of a skull. My mind automatically associates aircraft with raining death and destruction from the sky. This plane is different. It is taking me to Bill, the man I am going to marry, to my new home and my new country, America.

I am nineteen years old. Saying good-bye to Mama and Papa was the hardest thing I have ever done. I had to walk away from our house in the suburbs of Munich that had provided a happy home when my brother, Ludwig, and I were children and had sheltered my parents and me during the long, terrifying war years.

Ludwig was still a prisoner of war in Russia. I wouldn't be there when he comes home ... if he does. ... The Russians have yet to release most of their prisoners. I am torn between my family and the man I love. I had made my decision, but that did not ease the hurt deep inside me. Will I ever see any of them again?

We have our first glimpse of the English Channel below when we feel the plane turn. Soon there is an announcement that we are returning to Frankfurt because of motor trouble. In Frankfurt, we are allowed to stay on the plane, and it isn't very long before we are airborne again. We are flying across the English Channel, headed for Shannon, Ireland.

"I'm so glad we were able to get on the same plane," I tell Mariele. "It will be hard for me when I have to go on to Iowa without you."

"You'll do just fine, and remember we'll be able to call each other. Almost everyone in the States has a phone," she consoles me.

Mariele is lucky. Her parents are planning to return to the United States as soon as possible. My parents promised to come and visit me, but it may be a long time before they can get permission to travel. First of all, Ludwig has to come home. ...

For Mariele, to land in New York will be like a homecoming. She has lived in New York for ten years, knows most of the relatives there, and speaks and writes the language fluently.

For me, New York is a strange city, and the only person besides Mariele that I will know is my maternal grandmother, *Grossmama.* But I have not seen her since before the war. That was when she left for New York to visit her daughter Katherine, whom I barely remember from her visit with us in Germany when I was four years old.

When we arrive at the airport in New York City, people around us speak English so fast that I can't understand a word. Finally, Mariele and I are finished with customs and go out to the visitors' area where Aunt Katherine, Uncle Joe, and Mariele's fiancé, Frank, are waiting for us. My fiancé, Bill, had written me that he would not be able to meet me in New York. However, I feel sure that that was a little white lie because he wants to surprise me. But as I look around, I don't see him. I suddenly feel totally alone amid all the welcoming around me. It is hard to hide my disappointment.

Our first stop is Frank's mother's house, where Frank's whole extended family has congregated for a delicious meal with a great variety of Italian dishes and several bottles of wine. The conversation is flowing and is so animated that it seems as though everyone is talking at the same time. Mariele and I are told over and over how happy they are that we have finally arrived. What a great welcome! But these people are our family and friends. How will strangers react to us? No peace treaty with Germany has been signed. Legally, we are still the enemy. Will our new country accept us?

It is late in the afternoon when we drive to Aunt Katherine's home where I finally meet my cousin Joey. Even though he is two years younger, he is taller than I am. He is handsome, with dark wavy hair and a happy smile. We hit it off immediately. *Grossmama* looks a lot older than I remember her, but then why shouldn't she? It has been ten years since I last saw her. In spite of the lapse in time and the distance that had separated us, we greet each other warmly and renew our bonds of relationship.

At dinnertime, no one is hungry so we have a light snack and something to drink. It has been a long trip and a full and exciting, but exhausting, day. Mariele and I are grateful when Aunt Katherine shows us to the downstairs bedroom and bathroom we are to share. Cousin Joey has already placed our luggage in the room. We unpack only what we need for the night. Even though we are tired, it does take us a while to unwind and get to sleep.

The next morning, I awaken to the radio playing a song about shining shoes with Shinola®. Puzzled, I look at Mariele.

"That's a commercial. Companies pay to have their products advertised on the radio," Mariele explains.

"You mean Aunt Katherine doesn't have to pay five marks for each radio, like we did in Germany?"

"That's right."

"Gee, that's pretty neat."

"We better get ready for breakfast. I remember Aunt Katherine doesn't like to wait for people when it comes to mealtime."

Grossmama and Aunt Katherine are already at the breakfast table. Uncle Joe had left for work earlier, and Cousin Joey was at his summer job. He is earning money for college, I'm told.

Breakfast is another surprise. The butter is salted. Why put salted butter on bread and then put sweet jelly or honey over it? What a waste of precious butter.

After breakfast, Aunt Katherine asks Mariele and me to follow her as she heads downstairs, razor in hand. She takes us into the bathroom and proceeds to tell us:

"As I told you yesterday, we're having a cook-out today. All of our relatives, as well as some of our German friends, want to meet you. In America, we shave under our arms and our legs. Here is a razor. You better shave before our guests arrive."

I was relieved. For a fleeting moment when Aunt Katherine, a stranger to me until yesterday, started down the stairs with a razor, I thought back to Germany. After the war, sometimes girls who dated "Amis," American soldiers, were attacked and had their heads shaved. But I was in America now, and even though I thought only call girls and movie stars shaved in Germany, I shaved.

About noon, the relatives begin to arrive. Every family brings something to eat. I can't believe my eyes. So many people and such an abundance of food. In Germany before the war, we sometimes had a few relatives in for special occasions, but never this many. We also did not have neighbors or friends over for dinner. Most often, relatives would be invited for cake and coffee or tea. Should people be invited for dinner, they would bring the hostess flowers, a box of chocolates, or a bottle of wine. Here, it seemed, the relatives and friends bring part of the meal.

Meeting all of the new relatives was overwhelming. The cousins about my age seemed so young, bubbly, and carefree. At nineteen, I felt oddly old and sober. I was in the middle of so many new and overwhelming impressions on that first day that it finally came to me what I had done and how far from home I really was. Everything was strange and foreign. Mariele was introducing Frank to all of the relatives, so I took refuge and talked in German with *Grossmama,* who knew even less English than I.

When it was time to eat, one of Uncle Joe's nephews, Ben, followed me to the food table and explained the different foods to me, then took a seat next to me at one of the tables. For the rest of the party, he didn't leave my side. He was polite, nice looking, and seemed sure of himself. Home from college, he had been admitted to law school. He, too, had a summer job. He was careful to speak slowly, and it was easy to listen to him.

After the guests had left, I was drained. None of Uncle Joe's relatives spoke German, so I had been speaking and listening to lots of different English speakers. I was mentally exhausted. Translating for the Military

Government had been totally different. I was relieved to hear that tomorrow evening we were invited to Aunt Katherine and Uncle Joe's friends where we could talk German.

The next morning after breakfast another surprise awaited us. Aunt Katherine took us shopping. We went shopping in the car! Such luxury! The stores were full of merchandise, and there was such a great selection of goods in all sizes and colors it was confusing. Anything one could possibly want was available, and no one had to stand in line. The clerks were very friendly and didn't hurry us.

Aunt Katherine asked me to pick out a bedspread as a wedding present for Bill and me. I can still see it in my mind. It was white chenille, with the design of a big basket of flowers in pastel colors in the center and a border around the outside edge. The saleslady not only put the bedspread in a nice box with tissue paper and the store's name imprinted, but also put the box in a shopping bag, again with the store name in big letters. Such abundance, such luxury!

We came home with many shopping bags, and Uncle Joe took our picture to commemorate our first shopping trip in the United States—another almost dreamlike experience. ...

The next day, Aunt Katherine took us along to the grocery store, again by car. It seems everyone drove a car. I didn't see any bicycles. In the few days I had been in the United States, I'd had more rides in a car than in all the years I lived in Germany.

Not only were the store shelves full, but there also were different brands of everything and various sizes of each brand. No one cared how many things one bought. At the checkout counter, a young man who was just standing around started to take our groceries. I quickly reached for them, but Aunt Katherine stopped me, laughed, and said: "He's just going to carry them out to the car. That's his job."

I couldn't believe it. Not only do they let you buy whatever you want, and provide bags for everything, but they even carry the bags to your car. Only in America. ...

I also was struck by the fact there were no fences in Aunt Katherine and Uncle Joe's neighborhood, and during the day the house door was not locked. Such openness and trust!

In just a few days, I was living in a totally different world. I wanted to tell Mama and Papa and wished they could be here to experience this life so far removed from fear and the aftermath of a long and devastating war.

I sat down and wrote them a long letter pouring out my initial impressions of life in America.

One afternoon after Uncle Joe came home from work, he announced: "Let's not waste this beautiful afternoon. Get ready. We are going to Coney Island."

Joey also invited a girl from his class and Ben to come along. Mariele's fiancé, Frank, came to pick up Mariele and in two cars we headed out for Coney Island.

After arriving, Uncle Joe stopped at an ice cream vendor's stand. "Well, Anneliese, how many scoops do you want?" I didn't understand scoops. Pointing to an advertisement of an ice cream cone he gestured: "Ice cream, how high? Three, four, five?"

Ice cream was something we hadn't had for years, so I said, "Five high."

"You heard the young lady. She wants an ice cream cone 'five high.' Can you do it?"

"I can sure try," was the amused vendor's reply.

We all watched as he skillfully piled five scoops on a big cone, and everyone was laughing as I carefully balanced my "five-high" ice cream cone. The ice cream vendor handed Uncle Joe a paper cup, "Just in case," he laughed.

We had lots of fun. People seemed so carefree and happy that their joy was infectious.

After a while, Uncle Joe told us the fireworks would start soon, and we went to find a seat. The display of colors was spectacular, but the loud explosions reminded us of other times, and unwilling tears were streaming down Mariele's and my face.

Uncle Joe and Aunt Katherine realized the fireworks were too much for us, and so we left halfway through the display. ...

Editor's note: Ordering information for the autobiography
Christmas Trees Lit the Sky:
Growing Up in World War II Germany
by Anneliese Heider Tisdale
234 pages, AuthorHouse, 6 x 9 in., $27.99 hardback, $16.95 soft cover,
$3.99 Amazon Kindle E book

A State-by-State Look

California

German immigrants Hans and Erika Bandows made their way from New York City to California to operate a lodge.

It was 1969, and it was a fierce winter at Big Bear Lake. When the next fall rolled around, the Bandows wanted to throw a German party to thank their new clients and friends. That was Big Bear's first Oktoberfest, a festival that now runs for six weekends and that AOL rates as the top Oktoberfest in Southern California. Hans Bandows is still the Bergermeister for the Oktoberfest. The event is produced by Monica Marini, his daughter.

Big Bear Lake Oktoberfest photo

Folk dancers in native costume perform at Oktoberfest in Big Bear Lake, California. The festival was started in 1969 by German immigrants Hans and Erika Bandows.

One of California's most prominent Germans was Johann August Sutter, who immigrated in 1835 and began the Gold Rush in 1849.

Adolph Sutro, a native of Prussia, became mayor of San Francisco in 1894. Another immigrant, Arnold Enthe, took the only historical photographs of Chinatown before the 1906 earthquake.

Karl Freund was a famous cinematographer in Austria before coming to Hollywood in 1929 and filming such classics as *Dracula* and *Key Largo.* Arguably the most famous German émigré is Arnold Schwarzenegger, who emigrated from Austria to Hollywood, where he had a tremendously successful film career before being elected governor of California.

Dakotas

German immigrants, many of them wheat farmers, came to the Dakotas in the late 1800s, lured by promises of cheap land. Among the immigrants were Germans who had been living in Russia since the 1760s. A hundred years later, they came to the United States to avoid compulsory military service and to preserve their German culture. They formed close-knit communities, churches, and schools, where German was the primary language until World War I. The settlers also brought from Russia their knowledge of sugar beets and made them into a major crop of the Dakotas. Today, almost fifty percent of North Dakota residents and more than forty percent of South Dakota residents claim German ancestry.

Florida

The Germany Pavilion is one of the many national pavilions circling the 40-acre World Showcase Lagoon at the EPCOT Center at Walt Disney World Resort in Orlando, Florida. The Germany Pavilion has a glockenspiel with a sculpture of two doll-like, whimsical children, a contrast to the three solemn Hapsburg emperors gazing down from the height of eighteen feet. A statue of St. George and the Dragon stands in the center of the Platz (square). Traditional German architecture lends charm to the displays of German crafts and products, including fine porcelain, dolls, Hummel figurines, cuckoo clocks, beer steins, and crystal wine glasses. The Biergarten restaurant offers food from all regions of Germany, from cold wurst and potato dumplings to pork in aspic and fresh-baked pretzels. A typical German cookie shop features baked goods, cookies, and gift tins.

Georgia

Early History
In Georgia history, German Lutherans from Salzburg first arrived in the colony in 1734. Only two people among the settlers already there—Benjamin Sheftall, a lieutenant for General James Oglethorpe, the colony's founder, and Sheftall's wife—spoke German and helped the German newcomers get settled.

More Germans followed, and the Rev. Johann Martin Boltzius founded the village of Ebenezer, which grew through farming and grist mills. German immigrant John Adam Treutlen, who went to school in Ebenezer, was a leader in the American Revolution and became Georgia's first elected governor in 1777. Other Germans, many of them indentured servants, settled in Fort Frederica in southern Georgia and helped defend that frontier against the Spanish in Florida. The archaeological remnants of Frederica are today protected by the National Park Service.

Atlanta
The German Bierfest in Atlanta, now in its tenth year, is the only such festival in Atlanta. The festival, held in August in Woodruff Park, offers a large selection of German beers, plus German music and food.

Helen, nestled in the Blue Ridge Mountains in northeast Georgia, was transformed from a dying mill town into a cheerful Alpine village in 1968. That was the year that three Helen businessmen decided to give their town a face-lift to attract tourists. They consulted artist John Kollock, who had been stationed in Germany while in the Army. He delivered watercolor sketches that served as a blueprint for the transformation.

The downtown was remodeled with cobblestone alleys and Old World clock towers. New buildings went up, complete with gingerbread trim. An eighteen-bell glockenspiel fills the town with popular and seasonal music several times a day. Shops offer crafts and European imports, and restaurants serve Bavarian fare.

Every month, Helen offers a festival such as Oktoberfest, Bavarianfest in May, Fasching (before Lent), and a *Christkindlmarkt* set up before Christmas. About two million tourists a year visit Helen.

The magnet at left (available at Penfield Books) shows Bauernmalerei, a style of folk art developed over hundreds of years by German-speaking folk artists in western Europe. Examples may be found in the Bavarian area of Germany, Austria, and Switzerland.

Styles depict regional differences. This example is by the late Helen Blanck, a noted Minnesota folk artist. She also excelled in the many styles of Norwegian rosemaling and Swedish dala painting.

Greater Helen Area Chamber of Commerce photo

Main Street, Helen, Georgia

Illinois

The great influx of German immigrants would sweep into Illinois in the 1830s and 1840s, many of them attracted by the rich farmland in downstate Illinois. Others stopped in Chicago to make money before moving on, but many of them stayed. By 1850, Germans were about one-sixth of Chicago's population and remained the city's largest ethnic group until the 1900s, when that spot went to the Irish.

Historian Christiane Harzig writes that the German presence in Chicago was "ubiquitous," with many German-language schools and newspapers. That ethnic identity became less prominent with the world wars of the twentieth century, though citizens of German ancestry continued to be involved in the city's politics and education.

Chicago

Workers begin putting the world's longest bratwurst on grills outside The Berghoff Restaurant in Chicago on September 15, 2011. The effort, part of the German restaurant's 26th annual Oktoberfest, ended in a record bratwurst forty-seven feet three inches long that weighed in at forty pounds. The accompanying fifty-foot-long bun required thirty-five pounds of dough. (The world's longest sausage, according to the Guinness World Records, was 36.75 miles long and was made in South Yorkshire, England, in 2000.) A number of Illinois cities and restaurants, including The Berghoff Restaurant in Chicago, hold Oktoberfest celebrations.

Downstate

Downstate, the Mississippi River town of Nauvoo was the "most German-speaking town in Illinois" at the end of the nineteenth century, with German farmers, business owners, and community leaders.

Teutopolis, in south-central Illinois, was founded in 1834 by German immigrants who moved from Cincinnati. And Belleville, south of Springfield, was the first important German commerce center in the state, with ninety percent of the city's population either German-born or of German ancestry in 1870.

World's longest bratwurst, The Berghoff Restaurant, Chicago

Indiana

Germans were the largest immigrant group to settle Indiana in the 1800s, and more than a million of the state's residents—about one-quarter of the population—claim German ancestry, the most of any nationality.

Fort Wayne

Four German societies joined together in 1981 to start Germanfest, one of the biggest and most popular of the city's summer festivals. Visitors are invited to enjoy the *Essen, Trinken und Gemütlichkeit* (eating, drinking, and a warm, wonderful time) that power the June festivities.

The four founding societies illustrate the strong German heritage of Fort Wayne. The Fort Wayne Turners were organized in 1865 as the Turnverein, with a focus on gymnastics. Today, the Turners sponsor physical education, civic, and social events.

The Fort Wayne Männerchor-Damenchor is the second-oldest singing society in Indiana. It was founded in 1869 by immigrants who wanted to preserve and foster the tradition of German choral music. It continues to perform at a wide variety of events and also has toured Germany.

The Fort Wayne Sport Club grew out of the German love of soccer. The club was started by the many soccer players who came to the Fort Wayne area after World War II. In the beginning, the soccer teams were supported by local corporations. The soccer players wanted their own program, so they formed the club in 1927. It continues to sponsor recreational and competitive soccer, for ages four to thirty-plus, as well as social events.

The German Heritage Society, formed in 1986, is the most recent addition to the roster of clubs promoting German heritage and culture in Fort Wayne, "this most German city." The society sponsors cultural events, provides scholarships to study German, and promotes travel to Germany. The society also helped establish a sister city relationship between Fort Wayne and Gera, Germany.

Indianapolis

The Indiana German Heritage Society is headquartered in the historic Athenaeum Building—also known as Das Deutsche Haus, or The

German House—in Indianapolis. The society offers documents, books, and artifacts about the city's German heritage. Society members, familiar with the Old German Script used until 1930, hold reading sessions and translate documents passed down in families. The society presents Oktoberfest downtown. The German-American Klub presents an annual Oktoberfest in September in German Park on the south side. The Upland Brewing Company presents yet another one.

Jasper

The city and surrounding Dubois County are rich in German heritage, with the first German immigrants arriving in 1836. The majority of the first two hundred immigrants were from northern Baden, primarily from the small village of Wagshurst. All were Catholic.

Jasper Strassenfest photos

Crowds gather outside the Dubois County Courthouse in Jasper, Indiana, for the annual Strassenfest.

Revelers toast the opening of the Jasper Strassenfest.

An accordion and Lederhosen *light up the Strassenfest parade in Jasper, Indiana. The early August festival is in its thirty-fifth year.*

Soon after the first settlers arrived, the Bishop of Vincennes sent a Croatian missionary priest, Father Joseph Kundek, to serve the population. He founded St. Joseph Parish in 1837. The first settlers were poor and homesick, so Father Kundek decided to advertise in Germany and in German language newspapers in the United States for more settlers.

A large group from Pfaffenweiler, in south-central Baden near Freiburg, began settling in Jasper in 1847. The migration continued for decades. Another one hundred fifty came from Pfaffenweiler, and another thirty or so from the village of Reute, near Freiburg.

As Jasper grew, Father Kundek founded the nearby German communities of Ferdinand, Celestine, and Fulda.

He also asked the Benedictine order in Einsiedeln, Switzerland, to send Benedictine monks and priests to the area. The Benedictines soon after founded a monastery and seminary in nearby St. Meinrad.

Thousands of other Germans, both Catholic and non-Catholic, settled in Dubois County. Lutherans from villages near Bayreuth and Pegnitz in Bavaria settled in the northern part of the county. A large group of German Methodists and Evangelicals from northern Westphalia and southern Hanover, especially from the village of Ladbergen, settled in the southwestern part of the county. A large group of immigrants from Dudenhofen in the Palatinate settled in the southeast part of the county near Ferdinand. Hessians settled the central part of the county.

New Harmony

The Harmony Society founded Harmony as a communal, utopian society in 1814, but ten years later sold the property and returned to Pennsylvania. Robert Owen, a Welsh social reformer, bought the town and renamed it New Harmony. He, too, envisioned a utopian society, an experiment that failed for money reasons a short time later. The town continued its progressive ideas, however, opening a free public library and a school system open to girls as well as boys. Many of the town's historic buildings have been preserved. Paul Tillich, a well-known German-American existentialist philosopher and theologian, dedicated a park there that bears his name in 1963.

Harmony Society 1805 barn

Iowa

Fred Oehl photo

Historic Amanas, Sunday 1905

The Amana Colonies

Seven villages nestled in the rich farmland of Iowa County make up the Amana Colonies, a National Historic Landmark and one of America's historic utopian societies in the rolling hills of the Iowa River Valley. Hundreds of thousands of visitors annually visit the Colonies' restaurants, which offer menus heavy on German food that is served family-style, and the dozens of craft and curio shops that line village streets. The villages—just off Interstate 80 west of Iowa City—also offer meat and coffee shops, a furniture factory, antique stores, an old woolen mill, a bakery, a championship golf resort, a general store, wineries, and a brewery. The Colonies host annual Maifests and Oktoberfests, a Renaissance Festival, and a Cajun/Zydeco Festival in May. Village strolls, food sampling events, and art and craft shows also dot the active calendar that makes the Colonies a major tourist destination in Iowa. (Event details are at www.amanacolonies.com.)

The Amana Colonies' history begins in 1714 in southwestern Germany in the middle of the Pietism movement, when Eberhard Gruber and Johann Rock began the Community of True Inspiration, advocating the renewal of faith through reflection, prayer, and Bible study. Those beliefs brought persecution, and they relocated to central Germany. The community—numbering twelve hundred people and calling itself the Ebenezer Society—bought five thousand acres near Buffalo, New York, and relocated there in 1843–44. When more land was needed, the Inspirationalists looked to Iowa and the Iowa River Valley

Joan Liffring-Zug Bourret photo
An elderly Amana member of the Community of True Inspiration

for inexpensive, rich farmland with bountiful wildlife, timber, and water. The society arrived in Iowa in 1855 and chose the name "Amana"—"to remain true"—from the Song of Solomon Chapter 4, verse 8. Christian Metz relocated to Iowa in 1855 to assist in the founding of the Amana Colonies. They settled into twenty-six thousand acres, forming six villages about a mile apart: Amana, East Amana, West Amana, South Amana, High Amana, and Middle Amana. The seventh village, Homestead, was added in 1861 to give the villages access to the railroad. Those living in the communal society received a home, medical care, meals, household necessities, and schooling for children. Women of the Colonies prepared meals in fifty communal kitchens, supplied by huge gardens, orchards, and farms.

A Council of Brethren assigned jobs to the adults. Everyone attended church eleven times a week, with quiet worship during the day. Farming and the production of wool and calico supported the community, with others turning out well-made furniture and clocks, which became a hallmark of the villages. In 1932, during the Great Depression, the Colonies set aside the communal way of life. The Amana Society was formed to manage the farmland and larger businesses. Private businesses were encouraged. By adapting, the Colonies survived "The Great Change."

The villages today offer scenic vistas, trails, historic brick, stone, and wooden houses, and big vegetable and flower gardens. The Amana Heritage Museum in Amana tells the story of the Colonies' settlement and success.

Maifest, Amana, Iowa

Celebration Attire

German descendants across the nation honor their heritage by wearing *dirndls* and *lederhosen* at festivals.

Women in the communal Amana Colonies in Iowa wore long dresses and sunbonnets when gardening but never *dirndls.* Boys and men did not dress in *lederhosen.*

Allison Momany and Emilie Trumpold are shown (on the back cover) wearing *dirndls* at the Maifest in the Amanas. The photo on the back cover is by Emilie Hoppe. The Amana people were never Amish.

Jordan Heusinkveld

—71

A Word About the Old Order Amish
Settlements may be found in Pennsylvania, Ohio, Iowa, Kentucky, Illinois, and Wisconsin.

The Old Order Amish—of the horse-drawn buggies and homes without electricity—can be found to the south in the area around Kalona and Bloomfield, Iowa, and to the north near Hazleton, Iowa, and western Clayton County. The Mennonites and the Amish, like the Inspirational-ists, came to Iowa in the mid-1800s to follow their own religious, separatist teachings. Many are pacificists, opposed to war as well as infant baptism. Each Anabaptist group has a distinct heritage. Old Order Amish people and Hutterites in the Dakotas, Montana, and Canada speak a dialect of the German language. They farm and produce crafts.

Joan Liffring-Zug Bourret photos

Amish children wear the same styles of attire as adults.

72—

Davenport

Wherever civilization touches down, a German is close behind.

—August Richter, 1917

Geschichte der Stadt Davenport (History of the City of Davenport)

The German American Heritage Center & Museum in Davenport is a charming and informative tribute to the strong German influence that helped build this Mississippi River city.

The four-story, thirty-five-hundred-square-foot museum was put in a building built in 1862 by German immigrant Charles Hermman.

The building eventually became a thirty-room hotel and was a popular stop for German immigrants and farmers. Owner John F. Miller renamed the hotel Germania House around 1873, and the Gasthaus lasted into the twentieth century.

One popular display at the museum is a room that is restored to show what a hotel room looked like in the 1800s, complete with a narrow bed, a wash table, a chair, and a dresser.

"Many German immigrants coming from New Orleans or the East Coast stopped here to rest for a night until they could make contact with their families in other parts of the country," said Ruth Reynolds, the museum's administrative assistant.

The museum's third-floor permanent exhibit tracks German history and the German immigrant experience. The exhibit begins with a ten-minute film. Period clothing is on display. A trunk helps visitors imagine what it was like to pare one's possessions to one trunk.

A popular and moving interactive exhibit—"Step Into My Shoes"—traces the immigrant experiences of nine people, based on their diaries and historical information. The life stories are voiced by actors, with a video showing pictures of the people and the places mentioned.

Another outstanding collection is of zithers, a stringed instrument popular with German Americans and used to produce Hausmusik, or as several German Americans joke, "I've-had-a-few-beers farmer music."

Zither concerts are presented throughout the year, including around Christmas, and the instrument is enjoying something of resurgence in the Quad Cities: Davenport and Bettendorf, Iowa; Moline and Rock Island, Illinois.

The renovation of the abandoned hotel into a museum is a testament to German American organization, thriftiness, and fundraising,

The German American Heritage Center

museum volunteers say. Many dedicated hands worked to save and remodel the museum building, listed on the National Register of Historic Places. As the last German immigrant "guest house" left in the Quad Cities, this Heritage Center above, is an excellent example of High Victorian commercial architecture. The German American Heritage Center, formed in 1994, bought the old hotel in 1995. Fifteen years and $3.5 million in fundraising efforts later, all public floors of the building have been completed. Two galleries offer several temporary exhibits throughout the year. Current events and attractions can be found on the website www.gahc.org.

Further fundraising, remodeling, and exhibits have followed, as has a quarterly newsletter, The *Infoblatt.* A first-floor gift shop offers books and German collectibles: ornaments, pyramids, nutcrackers, and glass.

Memorial stone, above, and statue, Lady Germania, right, at the museum

John Johnson photos

Zither players from the German American Heritage Center & Museum in Davenport perform a Sunday afternoon concert at the Homestead church, now a museum of the Amana Heritage Society. Zithers were a popular instrument with German immigrants.

Schuetzen Park

Another interesting German heritage stop in Davenport is Schuetzen Park at 700 Waverly Road. In 1870, the area was a "shooting park," or a target range where people could practice marksmanship. The park also included an inn, dance hall, music pavilion, zoo, bowling alleys, roller coaster, athletic field, and picnic grounds.

The park's popularity began to wane around 1917 because of the anti-German sentiment accompanying World War I. The park was renamed Forest Park, and the Davenport Schützen Verein became the Davenport Shooting Association. The beginning of Prohibition in 1919 meant the end of beer and alcohol in the park.

All that remains of the park today is parkland with walking trails. The only original park building still standing is the 1911 streetcar station, which was named a local historic landmark in 1998 by the city of Davenport. Schuetzen Park artifacts and memorabilia can be viewed in the atrium of Heritage Court at the park, 3401 Schuetzen Lane.

Algona

The Camp Algona POW Museum in Algona preserves the history of a World War II prisoner-of-war camp that housed more than ten thousand German prisoners between April 1944 and February 1946.

The prisoners helped farmers—planting and harvesting crops, working with livestock, milking cows—in Iowa and southern Minnesota. They built bridges and roads, worked in logging and in factories—basically any job that needed doing, given a U.S. work force depleted by the war. They were paid ten cents to eighty cents an hour for their work.

The four-thousand-square-foot museum contains a model of the camp, photographs, artifacts, maps, and POW uniforms. Interviews with former POWs are available. Thousands come every December to view the Nativity scene made by the POWs. The Nativity contains sixty half-life-size figures. Architect Eduard Kaib and other prisoners fashioned the figures out of concrete over wire-and-wooden frames, and then painted the figures. Over the years, Kaib and other POWs returned to see the Nativity and tell of its creation. Kaib's 17-year-old granddaughter, Lorenza, visited the museum in July 2009 and was quite moved to hear a recording of her grandfather talking about the Nativity. He had died in 1988, before she was born, and she'd never heard his voice.

Grundy Center

Like many counties in the Midwest, more than half the residents of Grundy County, in northeast Iowa, just west of Waterloo, claim German ancestry. Many of those residents in the county seat of Grundy Center trace that ancestry to the Ostfriesland area in northwest Germany, adjacent to the Netherlands.

Hundreds of Ostfriesen residents have visited Grundy Center in the past twenty years. The mayor of Krummhoern inked a partnership between the two areas during a cross-cultural visit in 2010. The visits by the Germans give German Americans a chance to practice speaking "Low German" as opposed to the more formal "High German" taught in schools.

The Ostfriesian Heritage Society in Grundy Center maintains genealogical records at the library in Wellsburg and also sponsors a mixed chorus that sings in Low German, which sounds, not surprisingly, given the geography, much like Dutch.

The Hausbarn

Visitors to Manning can see a seventeenth century *Hausbarn*—a house and a barn—in this west-central Iowa city. The *Hausbarn* was built in 1660 by the Claus Thams family in Schleswig-Holstein in northwest Germany. University students helped take it apart and ship it to Manning. The structure was reassembled, complete with its wooden pegs, in Heritage Park, where it is open for tours May through October. The town also hosts an annual Oktoberfest, Kinderfest, and German King Shoot contest.

The *bauernhaus* shows how one thatched roof, once upon a time, covered both people and livestock. One end of the building was the family's living space, with an open hearth for cooking and warmth and a loft for storage. The other end of the building had a dirt floor and was for animals; it had large barn doors that allowed wagons to enter.

Also in Manning, the Leet-Hassler Farmstead has eight buildings preserved in their original form from the early 1900s. The farmstead is on the National Register of Historic Places. Manning's settlers mostly came from Schleswig-Holstein and Hanover, Germany, with their own German newspaper, *Der Manning Herold,* that circulated to other German communities in the state.

With the onset of World War I, however, the Iowa Legislature outlawed the use of foreign languages in public gatherings. English replaced German at school and at church, and *The Herold* started printing in English. The German Savings Bank changed its name to the Iowa State Savings Bank. It would be generations before those in Manning, and other communities settled by Germans, became interested in celebrating their heritage.

St. Lucas

The tiny town of St. Lucas in northeast Iowa opened the German-American Museum, Library and Family History Center in 2008 in what had been the former St. Luke's Catholic School building, built in 1911.

The handsome building, now on the National Register of Historic Places, houses several thousand historic documents, photos, books, and artifacts from the early days of German settlers in Fayette County. The St. Lucas Historical Society also sponsors an annual Oktoberfest and a Christmas Reflections program plus other events during the year.

Kansas

Newton

A statue of a Mennonite pioneer stands in Newton, Kansas, as testament to the Mennonite settlers who brought hard red wheat to Kansas from Russia, making Kansas the "breadbasket" of the nation.

The Mennonite faith started in the 1500s in the Netherlands, where followers were considered heretics and were tortured and killed. The religion spread, with many of the "quiet people" moving to Russia in the 1770s after Catherine the Great granted them land in the Ukraine and exemption from military services for a hundred years, as well as the right to practice their religion in peace.

At the end of those hundred years, the Russian military began requiring mandatory conscription, and about thirteen thousand Russian Mennonites decided to move rather than break with their pacifist faith. About eight thousand went to Canada, but many moved to Kansas, where land was cheap and similar to the steppes of Russia. They brought their best Turkey Red Wheat seeds with them.

The Mennonites would later found Bethel College in Newton.

Kentucky

Covington

Across the Ohio River from its bigger cousin, Cincinnati, is a smaller city of forty-two thousand. Covington, like that cousin, shares a deep German heritage. This city throws one of the nation's biggest and best Oktoberfests and also hosts a Maifest in May and an Original *Goettafest* in June. Germans came to farm in the Covington area beginning in the 1840s and then to work in the breweries in the 1890s. Many settled in Covington's MainStrasse neighborhood because it reminded them of the Rhine Valley in Germany. The five-block-long MainStrasse today offers shops and restaurants along cobblestone walkways. Most of the restored buildings date to the mid-1800s. Covington, along with neighboring Newport and Cincinnati, were regarded as the "German triangle" of immigration after the Civil War.

Out of that political milieu came William Goebel, the son of German immigrants, who was one of the first to support civil rights for workingmen, blacks, and women. He was elected Kentucky governor, only to be shot on the eve of his inauguration in January 1900, the only governor in U.S. history to be assassinated while in office.

Louisville

Most of the early German settlers came to Kentucky after landing in New Orleans and following the Mississippi and Ohio rivers upstream to settle in Louisville, St. Louis, and Cincinnati. By the 1850s, more than one-third of Louisville's population was German. By 1900, forty-eight thousand Louisville residents claimed German ancestry. Germans founded many of Louisville's churches and schools. They opened bakeries and dairies and also provided the labor at meatpacking plants in Butchertown and Germantown.

The Germans who immigrated after the failed revolution of 1848 were Marxists and atheists—a concept so foreign in Louisville that it led to riots as members of the Know-Nothing Party tried to block the new immigrants' ability to vote. German support led to the election of the first German-born mayor of Louisville in 1865, Philip Tomppert. The Germanic Heritage Society works to preserve their heritage in Kentucky and southern Indiana. A German-themed festival called the Original Butchertown Oktoberfest is held at St. Joseph Catholic Church.

Maryland

Baltimore

German immigration to Maryland started in the seventeenth century, with a large influx in the 1800s.

German Lutherans founded the Zion Lutheran Church in Baltimore in 1755, which still holds services in English and German. The German Society of Maryland was formed in 1783 to promote German culture and language in Baltimore.

Today, almost half a million Baltimore residents claim German ancestry, making it the largest ethnic group in the city.

One of the oldest German-themed festivals in the country is the German Festival held on the state fairgrounds in Timonium just north of Baltimore. It was scheduled to celebrate its 113th year in July 2013.

Among the festival's sponsors is the German Society of Maryland. Much of south Baltimore was settled by Germans in the 1800s, with "reminders of that heritage scattered throughout the city, in names such as the Otterbein community, Hanover Street, even Berger cookies," *The Baltimore Sun* reported.

And what better place for a signature Oktoberfest than Germantown? It was, anyway, until the festival outgrew the town's park and moved to High Point Farm in nearby Clarksburg.

Michigan

Frankenmuth, a city of ten thousand, is Michigan's "Little Bavaria." German food, architecture, Maypoles, a brewery, a glockenspiel, and German-themed festivals make visitors think they're ninety miles north of Munich instead of Detroit.

A band of thirteen Lutheran settlers, mostly farmers, founded Frankenmuth in 1845 in an effort to bring Christianity to the Chippewa Indians. They bought six hundred eighty acres of Indian reservation land for $1,700 from the federal government. More settlers arrived from Germany after journeys that required months of perilous travel. The pioneers eventually founded three other communities nearby, according to the Frankenmuth Historical Museum. They were Frankentrost in 1846, Frankenlust in 1848, and Frankenhilf, now Richville, in 1850. (The German word *Franken* represents the province

Pam Mossner photo

A celebrant toasts Oktoberfest in Frankenmuth, which is known as Michigan's "Little Bavaria." The city of ten thousand is known for its German food, festivals, architecture, and tourist attractions.

of Franconia in Bavaria; muth means courage.) Besides religion and farming, the settlers brought other occupations such as baker, bricklayer, blacksmith, lumberjack, and grain miller. In 1956, a local hotel was redecorated with a German look and given the name of the Bavarian Inn Restaurant to honor the community's German roots. In celebration, Bavarian Fest was born and is now one of Michigan's oldest cultural events.

The three-day festival in June features locally brewed beer, food, parades, folk dances, and Bavarian costumes. In 1990, in honor of the fall of the Berlin Wall, Frankenmuth initiated an Oktoberfest. The event, held in September, was given the official blessing of the city of Munich, Germany, in 1996. In 1997, the Hofbräuhaus Brewery shipped its beer outside of Germany for the first time to sell at Frankenmuth's Oktoberfest. The city now has one of only four Hofbräuhaus restaurants in the United States.

In addition, Frankenmuth hosts a Bavarian Easter celebration with colorful egg displays. A Volkslaufe, or People's Race, is held July 4. A Summer Music Festival follows in August, with polka bands and polka lessons. And the Christmas season is filled with tree-lighting, a candle-walk, carols, and shopping.

Minnesota

Following the United States' westward expansion, thousands of Germans headed west to Minnesota. And right into trouble. Welsh and Irish were already settled in the Minnesota River Valley in the 1850s when eighteen thousand Germans and twelve thousand Scandinavians arrived. The Sioux Indians were alarmed at the number of whites moving into their territory; they also were hungry, and they were angry over the way they were being treated.

New Ulm
In 1862, Sioux Chief Little Crow decided to take revenge. Government troops and five thousand Minnesotans were gone, fighting on the Union side in the Civil War. Little Crow's warriors took an oath to kill every white person in the valley. Most of the victims were German Americans. The warriors then turned to New Ulm, the heart of German settlement in Minnesota. The New Ulm townsmen held off the Indians, though twenty-six men were killed and nearly all the town's homes set on fire.

Government troops soon recovered the settlers the Indians had taken captive, tried 307 warriors for murder and rape, and moved the remaining Sioux to far-off reservations. A settler shot and killed the starving Little Crow in a berry patch.

Within months, New Ulm was rebuilt. Today, a monument on Center Street pays tribute to the New Ulm defenders. A statue on the town's highest hill honors an earlier hero, Hermann, who protected Germany in AD 9 from Roman legions.

More Minnesotans claim German ancestry than any other. And New Ulm, population thirteen thousand five hundred, is the state's most German city. It was a German immigrant, Frederick Beinhorn, a day laborer in Chicago studying English at night school, who founded New Ulm in south-central Minnesota in 1854. The carefully planned city was a place for the hundreds of German immigrants flooding the cheap labor market. The settlers built churches, schools, stores, and homes. Beer halls were never closed, even on Sunday, making New Ulm famous for its festivities.

The tradition of celebration continues today, with the Bavarian Blast in July, Oktoberfest in the fall, Christmas holiday events, Fasching (the city's version of Mardi Gras the weekend before Lent), and Schell's Bock

Fest (at the Schell Brewery) in May, among others.

The town also boasts a forty-five-foot-tall glockenspiel that chimes three times a day. The Concord Singers, a men's chorus founded in 1931, performs widely, and specializes in festive German music.

New Ulm abounds in German architecture, both commercial and historic, which is only fitting for "the most German city in Minnesota," as determined by a University of Minnesota study.

Turner Hall, completed in 1858, was destroyed in the Sioux War in 1862 and rebuilt in 1866 as a community center. It continues to serve that purpose and also is home to the Ratskeller restaurant.

The New Ulm post office, built in 1910 to resemble a town hall in Ulm, Germany, now houses the Brown County Historical Society. Dr. Martin Luther College, founded in 1884, boasts an impressive German-style building. The Cathedral of the Holy Trinity is a noteworthy example of German Baroque architecture.

New Ulm Convention & Visitors Bureau photo

Masked figures frolic during the Oktoberfest parade in New Ulm, Minnesota. The festival is held during the first two weeks of October and is modeled after the one in Munich, Germany.

Bemidji: Concordia Language Village

For modern-day immersion in German language and culture, youth, families, and adults can attend one-, two-, or four-week camps at *Waldsee,* the German Language Village of Concordia Language Villages near Bemidji.

Campers—or villagers as they are called—learn German by taking short classes and learning about German culture in simulations and programs. Additionally, villagers typically go *schwimmen* at the beach, bake tasty *kuchen* during activities, or play *Fussball* on the soccer field.

More than twenty-five thousand youth and adults have participated in *Waldsee* programs since 1961, and roughly six hundred participate each year.

Language Villages photos

Waldsee *has typical German architecture.*

To get the full experience, villagers at Waldsee *not only speak German, but also* eat *German. The kitchen is always cooking up tasty traditional German, Austrian, and Swiss recipes.* Spargel, *or* asparagus, *is a popular summer dish in the German speaking world, as well as at* Waldsee!

Waldsee *cuisine features German favorites.*

Twin Cities/St. Cloud

Elsewhere, many German immigrants settled in the Twin Cities—with a preference for St. Paul—and had more than twenty German-language newspapers over the years. In 1878, German Americans held fifty-four of St. Paul's fifty-seven brewers' licenses.

Another German historical footnote in Minnesota concerns alfalfa, a forage plant that no one was able to grow in the United States except in California.

Wendelin Grimm emigrated from Germany to Minnesota in 1857, bringing with him twenty pounds of alfalfa seed. He experimented for six years until he perfected the first winter-hardy strain of alfalfa and began distributing seeds of Minnesota Grimm alfalfa. It became the source of all modern varieties of alfalfa, which is now grown on an estimated twenty-five million acres in the United States. The Grimm homestead in Carver County, just west of the Twin Cities, is on the U.S. Register of Historic Places.

St. Cloud, about sixty miles northwest of Minneapolis-St. Paul, was another popular place for German immigrants. Many were attracted by the Catholic Church, which encouraged Germans to settle there. Large churches like St. Joseph's show German influence.

Northfield

At St. Olaf College, before Christmas, German language students and students from Germany join in a German Advent Service, *Adventsgoffesdienst,* featuring German Christmas carols, readings, and prayers in German.

Missouri

From nobility to peasants, thousands of Germans arrived in Missouri between 1830 and the mid-1850s. The greatest numbers settled in St. Louis, which was one-third German in 1850, and in the Lower Missouri River Valley, often called the Missouri Rhineland.

The immigrants established newspapers, theaters, libraries, churches, and schools that kept their language and traditions alive, with twenty German-language newspapers operating by 1900.

Many of the nineteenth-century immigrants created the wine industry along the Missouri River and what would become famous beer breweries in St. Louis.

As in other states, German language newspapers and institutions died out after World War I. Today, however, more than a quarter of Missouri's six million residents claim German ancestry, and the interest in German heritage is visible and celebrated.

Hermann

The people of Hermann met adversity three times and persevered. The first time, German immigrants in Philadelphia decided things were getting too "anglicized" and founded Hermann, about seventy miles west of St. Louis on the Missouri River, in 1837. They named their town for the German hero who held off the Romans in AD 9.

The settlers anticipated Hermann would be a competitor to St. Louis and thus made their Market Street ten feet wider than it is in Philadelphia. The town prospered and took seriously its mission to preserve the German language and customs.

Adversity struck a second time in World War I. Hermann sent its sons to war to fight for the Allies but felt the sting of the nationwide aversion to anything German, especially German language and customs.

The third setback came with Prohibition, from 1920 to 1934, which shut down the wineries and breweries that were a major source of the town's prosperity. To create jobs, the town attracted a shoe plant, but Hermann felt the Great Depression ten years earlier than other towns.

Among the places shuttered during Prohibition was the Stone Hill Winery, founded in 1847 atop a high hill with storage cellars cut into underground stone. The winery did not resume wine-making until 1965. Its wines have won numerous national and international awards,

Deutschheim State Historic Site captures the heritage of the German people who immigrated to Missouri in the 19th century. Open to the public as part of Missouri's Department of State Parks, the site offers guided tours of two historic 1840s houses in Hermann: The Strehly House (above) with print shop, home of the first German language newspaper west of St. Louis, and house winery, and the Pommer-Gentner House (below), a sterling example of high style German neoclassicism, furnished to reflect the early settlement period of the 1830s and 1840s.

and its Vintage 1847 Restaurant and spectacular vistas today attract thousands of visitors. Stone Hill also operates wineries in Branson and New Florence.

The Hermannhof Winery and its ten stone cellars are among the hundred buildings built before 1870 in Hermann that are now on the National Register of Historic Places. In total, seven award-winning wineries are within fifteen miles of Hermann and are part of the Hermann Wine Trail. Maifest (in May), Oktoberfest (in October), and Kristkindl Markts (in December) are major festivals in Hermann.

The clock tower was added to the old German School building in 1890. It is now the Historic Hermann Museum. Volunteers still wind the clock twice a week. The clock's mechanisms can be viewed on the second floor.

Bethel

In 1844, with Utopian goals, Wilhelm Deil, a German immigrant pastor, founded a religious communal society in Bethel on the banks of the North River in northeast Missouri.

Eleven years later, Keil decided the location was not "isolated enough." He left 340 members in Bethel and took 198 in wagon trains to found another communal society in Aurora, Oregon.

Aurora is now part of the Portland metropolitan area. Bethel, by contrast, remains an idyllic village with a population of a little more than a hundred, about forty-five miles west of Hannibal.

In the beginning, each family in Bethel had a home with a large plot to raise fruit, vegetables, chickens, hogs, and a cow. Money made from selling the products could be kept by the family. Feed for the livestock came from Colony farms, and goods from the Colony stores were delivered to every home.

Keil corresponded with his followers in Bethel but never returned to the Missouri settlement. The society disbanded after his death in 1877, with the nearly three hundred members dividing the money and property. More than thirty original Colony buildings survive, and the village was placed on the National Register of Historic Places in 1970.

The Bethel German Colony owns five of the historic homes, which are open for tours. The Bair home, built in 1845, is the oldest, with almost everything inside locally made.

A newly restored, white Victorian bandstand in the center of town is a stage for the Bethel German Band, a tradition that dates to settler days. The Colony hosts the World Sheep and Fiber Arts Festival, on

Labor Day weekend, one of the largest sheep and wool shows in the country, with sheep-shearing contests, dog trials, weaving and spinning contests, and plenty of lamb to eat.

A fiddle camp and contest is held in June, with competition in age categories. And a few weeks before Christmas, the village still welcomes the Black Santa, Knecht Ruprecht, who gives switches to bad children so they have time to mend their ways before St. Nicholas arrives.

The Fest Hall restaurant is open 362 days of the year, with German food to mark the big festival days, proprietor Dee Douglas says.

St. Louis

The German School Association is a Saturday morning language program in its 52nd year of operation in 2015. It has over 160 students, including classes for native German speakers. www.germanschoolstl.org

The German American Heritage Society preserves the German heritage, including scholarships. https://www.facebook.com/groups/gahs.stlouis/

The St. Louis German Cultural Society has a hall and hosts dances and events. www.germanstl.org.

Washington

On the southern bank of the Missouri River an hour west of St. Louis, Washington, has a distinct German flavor. It began as a ferry landing in 1822. By 1840, German Americans were about a third of the population, many of them Catholic Hanoverians from Osnabrück. St. Francis Borgia Church was founded by the Hanover immigrants.

The steamboat trade and the manufacturing of wagons, carriages, boots, shows, tanned leather, pottery, bricks, furniture, wooden shoes, and beer spelled prosperity for Washington before the Civil War. After the war, factories made zithers and corn cob pipes. Washington became "the corn cob pipe capital of the world," with a Corn Cob Pipe Museum now open for visitors. A number of wineries operate between Washington and nearby Hermann. Also, the historic John B. Busch Brewery—which closed during Prohibition, reopened, and then closed for good in 1953—is open for public tours.

The Spaunhorst House, built in 1869, is an excellent example of the brick houses built by early German settlers. Living history events are held throughout the year at the Kohmueller home, built by German immigrants from Osnabrück in 1879. And the Washington Historical Society runs a museum in the old Presbyterian Church.

Ohio

Ohio's rich farmland and waterways made it a popular destination for German Americans as America expanded westward. High birth rates in established German communities in Pennsylvania, New York, Maryland, Virginia, and the Carolinas made good land scarce and expensive. Native-born and German-born Germans came to Ohio through Maryland and West Virginia. Many Pennsylvania Germans settled in Canton, Massillon, Alliance, Steubenville, and other communities farther west. German families from the Mohawk Valley and Hudson Valley followed New Englanders to Ohio along the borders of Lake Erie.

The German Americans honored their origins by naming their new towns after cities in Germany—Berlin, Hanover, Strasburg, Dresden, Frankfort, Potsdam, Freeburg, and Winesburg. Other names bore witness to the religious roots of the settlers: Bethlehem, Nazareth, Goshen, and Canaan. Many of the settlers were farmers, but German laborers, craftsmen, and skilled professionals also came to the state.

Cincinnati

Oktoberfest Zinzinnati is the largest Oktoberfest celebration in North America, surpassed in size only by the festival in Cincinnati's sister city of Munich, Germany. Tens of thousands visit the September festival, which offers the full range of German food, including homemade goetta and pretzels. The Cincinnati Chamber of Commerce estimates eighty thousand bratwurst, sixty-four thousand sauerkraut balls, and eight hundred barrels of beer were served at the festival in 2010.

Oktoberfest starts with the official tapping of a keg of beer in each brewer's tent. Lots of German music highlights the festival, along with a beer barrel roll competition, a race featuring *dirndl*-clad waitresses carrying steins of beer, and a race for costumed dachshunds. The world's largest chicken dance closes each year's festival. The festival celebrates the city's deep German roots, including the impact on the brewing industry.

The German Heritage Museum in West Fork Park is a repository for historical artifacts and records of German American contributions to Cincinnati and the Ohio Valley. A log cabin from the 1840s was moved to the park and rehabbed to become the museum.

Cincinnati USA Regional Chamber photos

Beer and traditional food are all important at German festivals, especially at Oktoberfest. An estimated eighty thousand bratwurst were served at Oktoberfest Zinzinnati in 2010.

The building also showcases the activities of twenty organizations that make up the German-American Citizens League of Greater Cincinnati, founded in 1895.

In 1841, Cincinnati's population was twenty-eight percent German-American. By 1850, it was fifty percent. The hub of the German community was dubbed "Over-the-Rhine," an area across a canal from the main part of the city. The Cincinnati Volksblatt was published from 1846 until World War I.

David Ziegler, a German immigrant who had served in the Revolutionary War, became the city's first mayor in 1802. Immigrants faced discrimination, particularly those who were Catholic, in the 1800s until residents became more concerned about the extension of slavery in the South.

Andrea Fieler writes of being an immigrant in *My German Experience of Cincinnati*. She lived in Covington, Kentucky, across the river from Cincinnati. In Covington, she writes, she became accustomed to people calling her "hon, dear, and doll," which she found "kind of comforting and charming in this strange new country." That wasn't the case in Cincinnati, where she found "sounds way more familiar to my German ear."

Oktoberfest dancers in Cincinnati, Ohio

These two dachshunds attended the Cincinnati Oktoberfest. The breed is so popular it's called the national dog of Germany.

Columbus

Powerful reminders of German settlers can be found in Columbus' German Village: sturdy brick houses set close to hand-laid brick streets, slate roofs, carved stone lintels, clay chimney pots, iron fences, neat walkways, and heavy wooden doors.

Originally called South Columbus, the community was surveyed in 1814. Its residents founded St. Mary's Catholic Church, schools, a Lutheran seminary, Capital University, and many clubs and singing societies such as the Columbus Maennerchor that has been singing since 1848.

World War I, the Great Depression, and World War II all caused the village to empty out and decline. But its restoration, begun in 1960, has created the German Village Historic District, now on the National Register of Historic Places.

The village, separated by Interstate 70 from downtown Columbus, is now a vibrant neighborhood, with homes and shops in brick buildings that date from the 1840s. Annual house and garden tours testify to the revitalization of a once-abandoned area.

The village dropped sponsorship of its annual Oktoberfest in 2009, citing costs. The Schmidt family stepped forward with a subsidy, and the event now takes place at the Ohio Expo Center on the Ohio State Fairgrounds in Columbus.

Holmes County

In Holmes County, about fifty miles northeast of Columbus, are settlements of Amish and Mennonites, with German-themed restaurants and craft shops. Adjoining Wayne County also has Amish and Mennonites, whose ancestors came west from Pennsylvania.

Photo credit: DSCN4624 holmescountyamishbuggy e

An Amish couple ride in a horse-drawn buggy in rural Holmes County.

Zoar

Three hundred Separatists from Württemburg, Germany, founded Zoar in 1817, fleeing persecution after splintering from the Lutheran Church. After 1819, Zoar operated its fifty-five hundred acres and buildings on a communal system, with all resources pooled for the good of the community and with equal rights for men and women. Hard work, thrift, and the acute business sense of their leader, Joseph Baumeler, led to prosperity. By 1834, the community was debt-free.

Christmas in Zoar was just another work day until one Christmas morning when the locally made earthenware horn, used to call the people to work, shattered when blown in the bitter cold. The people took this as a sign from heaven that they should not work on Christmas Day.

Baumeler died in 1853. The coming of the railroad in the 1870s ended Zoar's isolation, and the nation's push toward industrialization and mass production hurt the village industries. In 1898, the society dissolved, with each member receiving $200 and fifty acres.

Today, Zoar has been restored to reflect its original simplicity and charm. A number of homes have been privately restored. Some have small shops, others are bed and breakfast establishments.

Buildings owned by the Ohio Historical Society and open to the public include the "Number One House," an 1835 two-story, Georgian-style house that was once the home of Baumeler and two other families; wagon, blacksmith, and tin shops; a formal community garden that covers the village square with a greenhouse; the Bimeler Museum; a general store built in 1833; and a bakery.

Events include a Harvest Festival in August, Christmas programs early in December, and art, quilt, and flower shows during the year.

Oregon

Mount Angel

One doesn't necessarily think of Oregon as a place to celebrate German heritage.

But Mount Angel, population a bit over three thousand and just north of Salem, throws a four-day, "Old World" Oktoberfest that draws hundreds of thousands of visitors and is cited as one of the nation's best. The festival has been going almost fifty years, and follows a tradition of community harvest festivals that began in 1878.

Nine German farmers settled in the Mount Angel area in the 1840s. One farmer reported he grew wheat seven feet tall. Another large influx of German immigrants came in 1890 to work in the breweries.

A group of German Catholic settlers arrived in 1867, led by Robert Zollner and his family, who came from Bavaria by way of Nebraska. The university-educated Mathias Butsch was so impressed with what he found in 1878 that he advertised for settlers in two Midwest German-language newspapers. The Catholic community had found its leader and Mount Angel its founder in Butsch. It wasn't long before the sound of the German language was common around the settlement and the Benedictines had opened an abbey, seminary, and monastery.

Today, the Oktoberfest features Bavarian dancers, oom-pah bands from America, Canada, and Germany, fifty Alpine food booths, street dances, a Biergarten and Weingarten, continuous entertainment on four stages, and a big road race/walk. Children perform a German weavers' dance every day at noon.

A huge glockenspiel, with life-size wooden carvings, sounds three times a day in Mount Angel.

By Hrystiv (Own work) [Public domain], via Wikimedia Commons

Charles Street in Mount Angel, Oregon

B & L Kister photo

A customer buys food from a booth at the "Old World" Oktoberfest in Mount Angel, Oregon. The small town, north of Salem, throws a four-day festival that attracts hundreds of thousands of visitors.

D Square Productions photo

This festival in Mount Angel is frequently cited as one of the nation's best.

Pennsylvania

William Penn was a great source of irritation to his father, Admiral William Penn, who was doing everything he could to disabuse his son of his attachment to the Quakers.

Everything he did failed, and when the elder Penn died, William Penn used his inherited fortune to buy forty-five thousand square miles of land, between Maryland and New York, from the king of England. His goal was to found a society based on equality and harmony, with freedom of religion and expression.

The Colony that Penn established in 1682 would become a magnet for the oppressed people of Europe.

Some of the first to accept Penn's offer were thirteen German families from the city of Krefeld. Originally Mennonites, they had converted to the Quaker faith. They arrived in Philadelphia on October 6, 1683, and founded Germantown just north of Philadelphia.

Of the later migrations, the largest number of Germans came from the war-torn Palatinate region. Others came from Württemberg, Baden, Franconia, Zweibrücken, Hesse, Hanau, Nassau, and Alsace. A considerable number came from Switzerland.

By 1750, German settlements were firmly established in southeastern Pennsylvania. The 1790 census found one-third of Pennsylvania's residents were of German origin.

The influx of Germans alarmed some of the English-speaking colonists. In 1717, Governor William Keith spoke of "great numbers of foreigners from Germany, strangers to our language and constitution."

A 1727 law asked all ship captains for lists of German-speaking passengers. Male immigrants age 16 and older had to sign an oath of allegiance to the king of England. In 1755, Benjamin Franklin expressed fear that Pennsylvania would be dominated by "Palatine boors."

The popular image of Pennsylvania Dutch people was men in black, wide-brimmed hats and beards and women in distinctive bonnets and long dresses—even though only a few dressed that way. The great majority of German-speaking people in eighteenth-century Pennsylvania belonged to the Lutheran and German Reformed churches.

In 1890, Philadelphia's German population reached seventy-five thousand, which exceeded that of even Milwaukee. Pittsburgh had thirty-seven thousand German-born residents in 1900. Other cities with large German populations were Erie, Reading, Wilkes-Barre, and Lancaster.

An ongoing debate concerns whether these people are "Pennsylvania Dutch" or "Pennsylvania German." Those favoring "German" point out that the people came from within the borders of what is now Germany. Others say that the term "Dutch" was an English form of the German "Deutsch." They point out that restricting "Dutch" to the language and people of Holland dates only from the nineteenth century. Today, many scholars agree that "Dutch" and "German" may be used interchangeably. Many simply refer to "Dutch" with no thought of windmills or wooden shoes.

The descendants of seventeenth and eighteenth century German immigrants largely assimilated into the American culture. The later arrivals, however, vigorously encouraged "German-ness." In 1835, the Männerchor, the first German singing society in the United States, was founded in Philadelphia. The city had German theaters and newspapers, and in 1915, more than two hundred German clubs.

German-speaking immigrants spoke a variety of dialects, with the Pfalz dialect, from the Palatinate region, dominating among the conservative "Plain Dutch." Efforts are being made by schools, universities, and some residents to preserve the language, with some churches holding annual dialect services.

The German Society of Pennsylvania was established in Philadelphia in 1764. Its library continues today with a large collection of German Americana. The Germantown Historical Society preserves the history of America's first German settlement.

Today, Germantown hosts the Germantown Revolutionary Festival with a re-enactment of the Battle of Germantown, the only Revolutionary War battle to be fought in Philadelphia.

Germantown visitors are never far from history, with a number of historic homes and buildings: St. Michael's Lutheran Church, where services were conducted in German until the 1920s; the Germantown Mennonite Meetinghouse; and the Germantown Church of the Brethren.

Many state, county, and local institutions work to preserve the Pennsylvania German culture. A listing of places of interest is maintained by the Pennsylvania German Society.

Places of Interest

Adams County

Gettysburg is the farm home of President and Mrs. Dwight D. Eisenhower and is open for tours. Tours begin at the National Park Service Visitor's Center near the Gettysburg National Cemetery. Eisenhower, the leader of the Allied forces during World War II, was of German heritage.

Beaver County

The Old Economy Village in Ambridge (second Pennsylvania home of the Harmony Society) is a National Historic Landmark that tells the story of the Harmony Society, one of the oldest successful religious communal groups in American history. With origins in Iptingen, Württemberg, the Harmony Society was established in Harmony, Pennsylvania, by George Rapp and about 500 members in 1805. These mystical pietists separated from the Lutheran church to return to the early Christian church. The Harmony Society site offers seventeen restored historic structures and sixteen thousand artifacts.

After ten years in Harmony, the Society moved to Indiana and built New Harmony, where they lived for ten years. They sold that town to Scottish social reformer Robert Owen and moved back to Pennsylvania, to build the town of Economy. They remained there until it dissolved with only two members remaining in 1905. The land around Economy was sold to the American Bridge Company, which formed the town of Ambridge.

The Harmonists believed that Christ would return in their lifetime, and that they were Christ's chosen people who would rebuild the Temple in Jerusalem to fulfill the prophecy in the Book of Revelations. They chose a life of celibacy to live closer to the teachings of the Bible and to be able to prepare for Christ's return without the burden of childrearing. The members remained German speaking and kept to German ways during their entire existence in America. Leaders only learned to speak English for business.

During the first half of the nineteenth century, the Harmony Society labored in agriculture and industry, forming three sustainable towns. Their pursuits included the manufacture of wool, cotton, silk textiles, and the production of wine, beer, whiskey, and cider, which they sold to the outside community. During the second half of the century, the Society turned to investing in railroads, coal, oil, lumber, and banking, as well as the development of the town of Beaver Falls, Pennsylvania, and its industries. The Society's wealth and philanthropy became well known throughout the Western world.

Top: *Lawns, arbors, and flower beds at The Old Economy Village in Ambridge, Pennsylvania.* Bottom: *The Rapp House Pavilion and gardens*

Berks County

This is the most German of all Pennsylvania counties. A mammoth Kutztown Folk Festival is held in Kutztown in early July, with June 28 proclaimed Pennsylvania German Day.

The Pennsylvania German Cultural Heritage Center at Kutztown University preserves thousands of artifacts relating to Pennsylvania German life.

The Heritage Center in Reading, is home to Gruber Wagon Works, a National Historic Landmark, the Wertz covered bridge, Melcher Grist Mill, and Der Distelfink. The center, which also offers relics and archival material, hosts an annual Heritage Festival in October.

Conrad Weiser Park in Womelsdorf has a home built in 1729 of a Pennsylvania German Indian who negotiated peace with the Iroquois tribe.

Northern Berks County

Barns in northern Berks County are decorated with colorful hex signs, particularly near Shartlesville, Hamburg, Shoemakersville, Virginville, Lenhartsville, Krumsville, and Kempton.

Butler County

Harmony, a National Historic Landmark, was founded in 1804 by Lutheran Separatists from the Stuttgart area in the duchy of Württemberg as the first American home of Johann Georg Rapp's Harmony Society. Influenced profoundly by the Book of Revelations, it became one of nineteenth-century America's most successful communal groups. The Harmonists left for southwestern Indiana Territory in 1814–15. Fifty years before the Harmonists, young George Washington visited an Indian village here on his mission to demand French withdrawal from the region, sparking the French and Indian War; a French-allied Indian shot at him, but missed.

Saxonburg was established in 1832 by brothers John and Frederick (Karl) Roebling from Mühlhausen, Saxony, Prussia. The Roeblings were eventually joined by more immigrants from their home province. John, an engineer, patented wire cable for suspension bridges. Roebling was contracted to build the Brooklyn Bridge, but it was finished by his sons after his death.

Zelienople was founded by Baron Dettmar Friedrich Basse of Iserlohn, Westphalia. In 1802, he purchased land and established the town he named for his daughter Zélie. Following their 1807 Frankfurt marriage, Zelie and Philipp Passavant came to Zelienople. Her father returned to Germany in 1818, but the Passavants stayed. Their youngest son, William, a Lutheran pastor, founded hospitals at Pittsburgh, Chicago, and Milwaukee; Thiel College; a Chicago seminary; and other institutions.

Photos courtesy:
The Harmony Museum

Woodcarver Gregg Kristophel demonstrates his craft at the Harmony Museum's Weihnachts-Markt (German Christmas Market) that brings thousands to the town every November.

The nine-site Harmony Museum is operated by Historic Harmony, a nonprofit historical society and preservation advocate. Regular guided tours involve three sites; some additional sites may be accessed independently and others by appointment; guided National Landmark District walking tours are offered by advance request. The museum is about twenty-two miles from The Old Economy Village, which commemorates the Harmony Society's third and final home.

Dauphin County

The State Museum of Pennsylvania in Harrisburg offers a large, well-organized collection of Pennsylvania Dutch arts and crafts.

The Museum of American Life in Hershey shows the culture of Pennsylvania Germans, the making of chocolate candy, and displays on Hershey's founder, Milton Snavely Hershey, born in Philadelphia to German parents.

Lancaster County

Medieval-looking buildings in Ephrata are all that remain of the eighteenth-century religious order started by Conrad Beissel, who emigrated from Germany in 1720. His sect wore white robes. Members advocated keeping the Sabbath on Saturday, the communal ownership of property and goods, and celibacy. The sect declined after Beissel's death in 1768 and the death in 1796 of the second leader, Peter Miller. The Pennsylvania Historical and Museum Commission maintains some of the Ephrata Cloister buildings.

The Landis Valley Village & Farm Museum in Lancaster offers a working eighteenth-century farm, with more than forty buildings.

Lebanon County

The Lebanon County Historical Society's Stoy Museum in the city of Lebanon offers period rooms and re-created shops.

The Alexander Schaeffer Farm Museum in Schaefferstown hosts a Harvest Fair on the grounds of a historic farmhouse that is a National Historic Landmark. The Brendle Museum offers classes in early American crafts.

Montgomery County

The Goschenhoppen Folk Festival in East Greenville is in mid-August. The Goschenhoppen Historians maintain several museums and a library and sponsor Pennsylvania German folk culture events.

The eighteenth-century farm of Peter Wentz in Center Point is preserved. It is listed on the National Register of Historic Places. The Folklife Museum and Library in Green Lane depicts local Pennsylvania Dutch culture before 1870 and includes weaver's, cobbler's, and turner's shops. The Montgomery County Historical Society in Norristown offers a small museum and library.

York County

The Hanover Dutch Festival is held in late July. The red-brick George Neas House, dating from 1795, is part of the Hanover Historic District and offers a glimpse into local culture and crafts.

Texas

Who knew? More than 10 percent of Texans—or 2.7 million people—claim German ancestry.

Germans were the largest European ethnic group to migrate to Texas, settling mainly in the Hill Country in central and southeast-central Texas.

The first German immigrants trickled into Texas during the Mexican period (1821–1836), lured by the Mexican government's offer of free land. In 1831, Friedrich Ernst and Charles Fordtran arrived in Texas, and Fordtran established the town of Industry, so named because of its quick growth.

Ernst wrote to a friend in Oldenburg, Germany, that Texas had "enchanting scenery and delightful climate similar to that of Italy, the most fruitful soil, and republican government, with unbounded personal and political liberty, free from so many disadvantages and evils of old countries." A newspaper published the letter, prompting more Germans to move to Texas. The letter may have overstated Texas' charms. Early immigrants fought in the Texas Revolution (1835–1836), battled Indians, and endured the hardships of a raw country where the weather was hardly identical to Italy's.

In 1842, the Society for the Protection of German immigrants in Texas, or the Mainser Adelsverein, was formed. Backed by noblemen and headed by Prince Carl of Solms-Braunfels, the Adelsverein encouraged immigration.

In 1844, three shiploads of immigrants arrived in Galveston and traveled down the coast to Carshafen (later named Indianola) only to discover the site had no living quarters. Camping on the wet beach in the winter, hundreds of immigrants died. More perished on the long trek inland to New Braunfels on the Comal River. From 1844 to 1847, about seventy-five hundred Germans arrived in Texas through the Adelsverein.

The society replaced Prince Carl with Baron Ottfried Hans von Meusebach, who arrived at Galveston in 1845. Dropping his title, he became John O. Meusebach. His fiancée, Elizabeth von Hardenberg, remained in Germany. They corresponded, but Elizabeth died. Meusebach later married a Texan, Agnes Coreth, who was originally from Austria.

The fierce Comanche were a constant threat to settlers. Realizing that three million acres between the Llano and Colorado rivers—the Fisher-Miller Land Grant—was claimed by Waco and Comanche Indians as their home, Meusebach first settled with the less hostile Waco tribe, and then arranged with a Comanche chief, Ketemoczy, for a peace council.

In January 1847, Meusebach rode into the Comanche camp with forty men. Several hundred warriors lined one side of the camp, armed with guns and bows and arrows. Females and children lined the other side, while the three head chiefs—Buffalo Hump, Santa Anna, and Mopechucope—sat in the middle on buffalo robes.

Meusebach and his men rode up and down the aisle of warriors, emptying their rifles in the air to show they were peaceful and unafraid. Impressed by that bravery, the Indians named Meusebach El Sol Colorado, the Red Sun.

For Meusebach's promise of three dollars' worth of presents, the Comanche agreed to allow the colonists to settle peacefully on the Fisher-Miller Land Grant. This became the only treaty between Europeans and Texas Indians in which both sides kept their promises.

Today, Texas "German Country" is a fifty- to seventy-five-mile swath around Austin, though German influence isn't limited to the Hill Country. Gainesville and Muenster, near the Oklahoma border, are German-American communities. San Antonio and Houston also have sizable German-American populations.

Among the towns with German names are New Braunfels, Fredericksburg, Solms, Hocheim, Westphalia, Oldenburg, Mecklenburg, New Berlin, Germania, Rhineland, New Baden, and Weimar. Others, such as Industry, Comfort, and Sisterdale, are German American in all but name.

Fredericksburg

Founded in 1846 by one-hundred twenty-five settlers, Fredericksburg was named for Prince Frederick of Prussia.

The city of ten thousand is about 75 miles from San Antonio. Its wide streets, latticed windows, *willkommen* signs, and German restaurants testify to its German heritage.

Sunday Houses are an unusual and historic attraction. When the city was first settled, farm families would travel some distance for Sunday church services. Rather than attempt the journey in the dark, they pitched tents to stay in town on Saturday night. Those tents were replaced with charming two-room houses, with second-floor lofts set aside for sleeping. Porches and gingerbread trim were added to the Sunday Houses.

The Weber House, an original Sunday House, is preserved at the Pioneer Museum. The Metzer and Rode Sunday Houses also are available for viewing in the city's historic district, which is listed on the National Register of Historic Places.

Some Sunday Houses have been turned into bed-and-breakfast accommodations. Visitors also can see the historic St. Mary's Church and the Vereins Kirche, an eight-sided community church that also served as a school, town hall, and meeting place.

The city's Marktplatz is home to the annual Oktoberfest. The three-day festival, held the first weekend in October, attracts seventeen thousand visitors for German food and thirty varieties of beer, oom-pah, polkas and waltzes, domino tournaments, and an "Oktubafest." Mexican-American and Cajun foods also are offered.

The city also hosts a St. Nikolaus Markt Holiday Festival, which features a thirty-foot lighted Christmas tree and a twenty-six-foot Christmas pyramid made in Germany. And for the past fifty years, the city has hosted a Night in Old Fredericksburg on the second weekend of June to celebrate its German roots and Texas history. The city also offers German restaurants, vineyards, and wineries.

Another attraction is The National Museum of the Pacific War, located in what was the childhood home of Admiral Chester Nimitz, the German-American who commanded the Pacific Fleet in World War II. (The nation's nuclear-powered aircraft carriers are named in honor of Nimitz.)

The admiral's grandfather, Captain Charles H. Nimitz, came to Fredericksburg in 1847 and built a series of hotels, each larger and more splendid than the last. The building now housing the Pacific War Museum was the last one he built. It included hotel rooms, a casino, saloon, general store, brewery, and stables, and was a stopping place on the road from San Antonio to El Paso. Among those who slept there: Robert E. Lee, Ulysses S. Grant, Rutherford B. Hayes, and a "Mr. Howard," better known as the outlaw Jesse James.

Admiral Chester Nimitz

The National Museum of the Pacific War, Fredericksburg, Texas

Chester Nimitz, the overall commander of the U.S. Navy's Pacific Fleet during World War II, was born in Texas, where he was greatly influenced by his grandfather, a former seaman in the German Navy. Nimitz, who served in World War I, assumed control of the decimated U.S. Navy after the Pearl Harbor attack, aggressively pushing back the Japanese. After the war, he became Chief of Naval Operations, shifting Navy submarines from diesel to nuclear power. The first nuclear-powered aircraft carrier is named for him. The museum is the site of his childhood home.

The legendary Fredericksburg Easter Fires have been a tradition since 1847, when Meusebach was negotiating the land treaty with the Comanches. During those talks, fires blazed on the hills overlooking Fredericksburg—the Indians' signal that all was peaceful. The fires frightened some children until one mother spun a tale, saying the Eastern Bunny and his helpers were cooking eggs in huge cauldrons and coloring them with wildflowers from the hills. Today, the pageant of the fires still heralds Easter, just like such fires in Germany.

Muenster

German Catholic settlers Carl and Emil Flusche, in 1889, founded Muenster, one of several towns the brothers would create in Texas. German was spoken until after World War I, when English became the language of choice.

The city of sixteen hundred, near Gainesville, has preserved German customs and produces traditional German foods at local meat markets and bakeries. It hosts a popular Germanfest every March, with lots of beer, German food and music, a bike rally, and fun runs. A Christkindlmarkt is held every year on Thanksgiving weekend.

In another nod to the area's German roots, the Muenster Hornets' high school football team plays the Lindsay Knights each fall in the annual Kraut Bowl.

New Braunfels

Founded in 1845 by Prince Carl, New Braunfels today offers German-themed festival, tree-lined streets, and beautifully preserved houses and buildings of original settlers.

The Sophienburg Memorial Museum stands where Prince Carl once had his fortified headquarters. The original Sophienburg, named after his fiancée, Princess Sophia of Salm-Salm, was destroyed by a storm in 1866. Museum exhibits include a hand-crafted model of the Prince's castle in Braunfels, Germany. The museum of Texas Handmade Furniture offers visitors an in-depth look at the art of furniture making.

Some restored historic homes are open to visitors. The Lindheimer home was built by Ferdinand Lindheimer, editor of New Braunfels' first newspaper, the *New-Braunfelse Zeitung*. Lindheimer, also known as the father of Texas botany, led the first colonists to the site that would become New Braunfels.

The Baetge house, built in 1852, features hand-hewn timbers and cypress siding. Carl Baetge, born in Germany, built a Russian railroad from St. Petersburg to Moscow to connect the Winter Palace to the Summer Palace. In New Braunfels, he built his home near Canyon Lake. The original home was dismantled, moved, and rebuilt at Conservation Plaza. The New Braunfels' Wurstfest takes place in late October, with bands, dancing, tent shows, and exhibits.

Stonewall

About fifteen miles east of Fredericksburg, near Stonewall, population 525, is the Lyndon B. Johnson State Historical Park and also the LBJ National Historical Park, both near the ranch where the thirty-sixth president was born and is now buried. The state park offers visitors a chance to see a two-room dogtrot cabin built by German immigrant H. C. Behrens during the 1870s, a log cabin built in the 1860s by the Danz family, and a Living History Farm at the Sauer-Beckmann Farmstead.

Tomball

German Heritage Festival photos

Tom Vistine plays at the German Heritage Festival in Tomball, Texas.

Tomball, population 10,000, is one of the many Texas towns settled by Germans who came through the Port of Galveston for the rich farmland near what would become Houston. In March, for the past thirteen years, the city has hosted a German Heritage Festival to celebrate the city's roots with German music, dance, costumes, food, and culture. It also offers Texas Germans a chance to practice speaking German—such as *"Willkommen, y'all."* Tomball's sister city is Telgte, Germany.

German Heritage Festival photo

Waylon Kidd, left, in native German dress, and James Thompson in a Royal Bavarian Guard uniform welcome visitors to the German Heritage Festival in Tomball, Texas. The festival offers Texas Germans a chance to practice speaking German—or "Willkommen, y'all," as the festival advertises.

A Texas-German-Indian Story

Herman Lehmann lived with his German immigrant family about twenty-five miles northwest of Fredericksburg. He was 11 years old when captured by Apache Indians in 1870. His younger brother, William, also was captured but escaped and made it home in about nine days.

But Herman would live among the Indians the next nine years before returning to his birth family.

At first, he said, he was treated harshly and tortured until members of the tribe decided to adopt him. He became an Indian, learning all the hunting and fighting skills that young male Indians had to learn.

When an Apache medicine man murdered Herman's chief and tried to kill Herman, Herman killed the medicine man. Fearing for his own life, Herman escaped. He lived on his own for about a year before joining the Comanche Indians.

When the Indians were rounded up and forced onto reservations, soldiers brought a reluctant Herman back to his family. He had a difficult time adjusting to wearing European clothes, eating cooked meat, sleeping in a bed, and not stealing.

Eventually, he was reconciled to his new life. He relearned German, married, and had five children whose descendants live on in Texas today. He nonetheless retained his Comanche ties, and the U.S. government considered him a member of the tribe.

Virginia

Staunton

The Frontier Culture Museum of Virginia in Staunton includes three farms depicting pioneer homes from Germany, Ireland, and England, the homelands for the majority of immigrants to the state.

Because many Germans who settled in Virginia came from the Palatinate area—some by way of Pennsylvania—the German farmhouse comes from the village of Hoerdt in the Germersheim district. A gift from the people of Rheinland-Pfalz, the farm depicts life in the middle of the eighteenth century. Costumed interpreters re-enact daily life.

The museum schedules celebrations for May Day and Oktoberfest, with events for children throughout the year.

Middleburg

The Christmas Sleigh store in Middleburg offers a vast array of German and Austrian products, including pyramids, music boxes, nutcrackers, Christmas ornaments, beer steins, cuckoo clocks, and party supplies. They are especially noted for their Easter eggs.

Washington

Leavenworth

By transforming into an Alpine German village, this mountain town survived. Founded in 1884, the city prospered for decades, but by the late 1960s had withered with the loss of railroad, sawmill, and other payrolls.

What to do? The University of Washington's Community Development Division came up with four ideas: Become a Wild West town, a New West town, a Danish-theme town like Solvang, California, or an Alpine German village. The residents chose the latter.

About twenty percent of those living in the state of Washington claim German ancestry, the most of any group. Today, Leavenworth, a city of two thousand nestled in the mountains east of Seattle, looks and acts truly Bavarian.

The edelweiss Alpine flower, transplanted from Germany, blooms throughout the city, as do colorful flowers. A twenty-five-bell carillon chimes every hour. German-themed restaurants and lodgings, house cheese, clock, and gift shops, and buildings decorated with gingerbread trim, also line the streets.

One of the popular attractions is the Leavenworth Nutcracker Museum. Opened in 1995, it houses more than six thousand nutcrackers from the collection of Arlene Wagner, who taught ballet and oversaw multiple productions of *The Nutcracker,* which spurred her interest in the collection.

Project Bayern helped form Musikkapelle Leavenworth, the town band, and also helped costume the Edelweiss Tanz Gruppe, the town's German dance group. It also helped build the town beer wagon and puts up the *Maibaum* (May pole) each May.

Visitors enjoy the Maifest, and the hugely popular Oktoberfest (that stretches over three weekends and only serves German beer), the Christkindlmarkt after Thanksgiving, and the Christmas lighting festival held during three weekends in December.

The city also hosts an international accordion event, a Bavarian Bike Race, and wine festivals.

Steven Pavlov photo

December snow on Front Street in Leavenworth, Washington. The building code only allows buildings with a Bavaria theme. Business owners greet visitors.

Leavenworth Nutcracker Museum photos

Artifacts are shown from the Leavenworth Nutcracker Museum in Leavenworth, Washington. Left: An antique wooden nutcracker is on display. Middle: Rare porcelain and ivory nutcrackers are displayed. Right: An 1880 miner of Wilhelm Füchtne, with a present-day Füchtne.

Oktoberfest in Leavenworth, Washington, features lovely Fräulein *to greet visitors. About a million tourists annually visit the city.*

Buildings in Leavenworth, Washington, have an Alpine theme.

Odessa

German-speaking settlers named this eastern Washington city after the Odessa region of Russia where they had grown wheat along the Black Sea and the Volga River.

Wheat remains the primary crop in the area, where life still revolves around *Kinder, Kirche*, and *Küche* (children, church, and kitchen).

The Odessa Deutschesfest in September features a German Biergarten, German food and music, and a Volksmärsch.

Wisconsin

Miss German-American Societies poses at German Fest Milwaukee.

Germans were so thoroughly entrenched in Wisconsin that when it entered the Union in 1848, its leaders tried (unsuccessfully) to make it a German-speaking state. In the proportion of German immigrants, Wisconsin led all states. The German settlers found the state's climate and soil similar to Germany's, and an immigrant could vote after living in Wisconsin one year. German churches, schools, and societies kept language and culture alive.

A crowd watches German folk dancers at German Fest Milwaukee. The festival celebrates the city's German heritage.

Many Germans heard about Wisconsin from relatives already settled there. Among the glowing reports were books written by Carl E. Hasse, Carl de Haas, and Ferdinand Goldman. The state printed pamphlets for distribution in New York and Germany. When Wisconsin was made a Catholic diocese in the 1840s, with a German-speaking bishop, more German Catholics came.

Most of the immigrants settled in the eastern and lakeshore regions, with Milwaukee a popular destination. About eight thousand Germans arrived in Milwaukee in the 1850s. In 1860, more than one-third of Milwaukee's forty-five thousand residents were Germans. By 1900, 34 percent of Wisconsin's populations claimed German descent.

Immigrants from Württemberg—with names like Schlitz, Pabst, and Blatz—started breweries that made Milwaukee beer famous. (The mansion that beer baron Frederick Pabst built in 1890—and which later became the residence of Milwaukee's archbishop—has been restored and is open for tours.) Across the state in La Crosse, the G. Heileman Brewing Company produced another famous beer until its acquisition in 1996 by Stroh's.

Every July, Milwaukee celebrates its German roots as the "Munich of the Midwest," with a huge German Fest on the lakefront. In four days of festivities, the crowds typically consume twenty thousand bratwurst, fifteen thousand slices of strudel, and ten thousand pounds of potato salad, according to German Fest Milwaukee Inc.

Old World Wisconsin, an outdoor living history farm about thirty-five miles southwest of Milwaukee, preserves the farmsteads and settlements established by European immigrants in the nineteenth century. The German area of the site features three meticulously restored farms, including a horse-powered threshing machine.

Watertown

In Watertown in southeast Wisconsin, Margarethe Schurz, the wife of the statesman Carl Schurz, started the first kindergarten in the United States in 1856. The kindergarten building was restored and moved to the grounds of the Octagon House, an eight-sided home built in 1854 that is now a museum in Watertown.

German Fest Milwaukee photo

These antique brass folk instruments, shown at the German Fest Milwaukee, were once used by oom-pah bands. The annual festival is held over four days in July on the city's lakefront.

German-American Museums

Here is a sampling of museums devoted to German-American heritage in the United States.

Georgia
– Georgia Salzburger Society, 2980 Ebenezer Road, Georgia Highway 275, Rincon, Georgia 31326. (912) 754-7001. georgiasalzburgers.com

Iowa
– Ackley Heritage Center, 737 Main Street, Ackley, Iowa 50601. (641) 847-2201.
– Amana Heritage Museum, 4310 220th Trail, Amana, Iowa 52203. (319) 622-3567. amanaheritage.org/museums.html
– German American Heritage Center, 712 West Second Street. Davenport, Iowa 52802. (563) 322-8844. gahc.org

Illinois
– Hegeler Carus Mansion, 1307 Seventh Street, La Salle, Illinois 61301. (815) 224-5891. hegelercarus.org
– Maeystown Preservation Society, c/o Postmaster, Maeystown, Illinois 62256. (618) 458-6464. maeystownpreservationsociety.org
– Dank-Haus German American Cultural Center, 4740 North Western Avenue, Chicago, Illinois 60625. (773) 561-9181. dankhaus.com

Kansas
– The Mueller-Schmidt House Museum, 112 E. Vine Street, Dodge City, Kansas, 67801. (620) 227-6791.

Kentucky
– MainStrasse Village, 406 West Sixth Street, Suite 201, Covington, Kentucky 41011. (859) 491-0458. mainstrasse.org

Louisiana
– German-American Cultural Center and Museum, 519 Huey P. Long Avenue, Gretna, Louisiana 70053. (504) 363-4202. gacc-nola.org
– Deutsches Haus, 1023 Ridgewood Drive, Metairie, Louisiana 70001. (504) 522-8014. deutscheshaus.org

Michigan
– Frankenmuth Historical Museum, 613 South Main Street, Frankenmuth, Michigan 48734. (989) 652-9701. frankenmuthmuseum.org

Minnesota
– Brown County Historical Society, 2 North Broadway Street, New Ulm, Minnesota 56073. (507) 233-2616. browncountyhistorymn.org

Missouri
– Deutschheim State Historic Museum, Museum at the German School, Hermann, Missouri 65041. (573) 486-2200. hermannmissouri.com

Ohio
– German Pioneer Museum, 4764 West Fork Road, Cincinnati, Ohio 45247 (513) 598-5732. gacl.org/museum.html
– German Village Meeting Haus, 588 South Third Street, Columbus, Ohio 43215. (614) 221-8888. germanvillage.com
– Bimeler Museum, P. O. Box 621, Zoar, Ohio 44697. (330) 874-3011. http://historiczoarvillage.com

Pennsylvania
– Landis Valley Museum, 2451 Kissel Hill Road, Lancaster, Pennsylvania 17601 (717) 569-0401. landisvalleymuseum.org
– Moravian Museum of Bethlehem, 505 Main Street, Bethlehem, Pennsylvania 18018. (610) 691-6055. historicbethlehem.org
– Harmony Museum, 218 Mercer Street, Harmony, Pennsylvania 16037. (724) 452-7341. harmonymuseum.org
– Pennsylvania German Cultural Heritage Center, Kutztown University, 22 Luckenbill Rd., Kutztown, Pennsylvania 19530. (610) 683-1589. kutztown.edu/community/pgchc/index1.htm
– Saxonburg Museum, 199 North Rebecca Street, Saxonburg, Pennsylvania 16056. (724) 352-3024. saxonburgpa.com/saxonburg-museum.html
– Zelienople Historical Society, 243 S. Main Street, Zelienople, Pennsylvania 16063. (724) 452-9457. zelienoplehistoricalsociety.com

Texas
– Pioneer Museum, 312 West San Antonio Street, Fredericksburg, Texas 78624. (830) 990-8441. pioneermuseum.net

Washington

– Leavenworth Nutcracker Museum, 735 Front Street, Leavenworth, Washington 98826. (509) 548-4573. nutcrackermuseum.com
– Upper Valley Museum at Leavenworth, 347 Division Street, Leavenworth, Washington 98826. (509) 548-0728 uppervalleymuseum.org

Wisconsin

– Chase Stone Barn Park, County Road, South Chase, Wisconsin, 54162. (920) 822-5447. townofchase.org
– Milwaukee County Historical museums (three of them):
–Milwaukee County Historical Society Museum, 910 N. Old World Third Street, Milwaukee, WI 53203-1591. 414-273-8288. milwaukeehistory.net
– Old World Wisconsin,W372 S9727 Hwy 67, Eagle, Wisconsin 53119. (262) 594-6300. http://oldworldwisconsin.wisconsinhistory.org
– Rhinelander Logging Museum, P.O. Box 658, Rhinelander, Wisconsin 54501. (715) 369-5004.
rhinelander-resorts.com/loggingmus/logging.htm

American Cities with German Names

This is a sampling of cities in the United States that have German names. And there are more than listed here. More than thirty U.S. cities and towns, for example, are named Berlin. Some accent the first syllable, and one (in Iowa) changed its name to Lincoln during World War I.

Connecticut	Guttenberg	Frankenmuth
Berlin	Hamburg	Frankfort
	Hanover	Westphalia
Iowa	Klemme	
Amana	Luther	**Minnesota**
Allendorf	Minden	Danube
Berlin	Reinbeck	Essig
Bettendorf		Flensburg
Davenport	**Michigan**	Fulda
Germantown	Bergland	Hamburg
Germanville	Hamburg	Hanover
Graettinger	Hanover	Heidelberg

Herman
Hoffman
Karlstad
New Germany
New Munich
New Ulm
Schroeder
Zimmerman

Missouri
Baden
Frankford
Freistatt
Hermann
New Hamburg
New Offenburg
Rhineland
Weingarten

Nebraska
Gothenburg
Herman
Holstein
Minden
Pilger
Steinauer
Manheim

North Dakota
Berlin
Bismarck
Bremen
Dresden

Hamberg
Hannover
Heil
Heimdal
Karlsruhe
Millbach

South Dakota
Frankfort
Kranzburg
Wagner

Ohio
Berlin
Bremen
Dresden
Germantown
Gnadenhutten
Hamburg
Hanoverton
Leipsic
New Bavaria
New Bremen
New Riegel
Steuben
New Bremen
New Berlin
Obernburg
Otto

New York
Angelica
Berlin

Dresden
East Otto
Fleischmanns
Frankfort
German
Germantown
Hamburg
Helmuth
Hoffmeister
Keeseville
Mannsville
Mecklenburg
New Bremen
New Berlin
Obernburg
Otto

Pennsylvania
Ackermansville
Angelica
Baden
Berlin
East Berlin
East Germantown
Fritztown
Germansville
Germantown
Hamburg
Hanover
Heidelberg
Hummelstown
King of Prussia
Kleinfeltersville

—121

Popular German Baby Names

Here are the most popular German baby names in 2013. 182,300 birth certificates were surveyed.

Boys		Girls	
1.	Ben	1.	Mia
2.	Luca	2.	Emma
3.	Paul	3.	Hannah
4.	Jonas	4.	Sophia
5.	Finn	5.	Anna
6.	Leon	6.	Lea
7.	Luis	7.	Emilia
8.	Lukas	8.	Marie
9.	Maximilian	9.	Lena
10.	Felix	10.	Leonie

Source: http://www.firstnamesgermany.com/

Here are some of the most popular German baby names from 1957 to 2000.

Boys	Girls
Bernd	Angelika
Christian	Anja
Dieter	Anke
Dirk	Brigitte
Dominik	Franziska
Eric/Erik	Heike
Felix	Ines
Jonus	Karin
Jörg	Katharina
Jürgen	Klaudia/Claudia
Klaus	Kristin/Christin
Maximilian	Monika
Niklaus	Sophia/Sophie
Ralf/Ralph	Ursula
Tobias	Uta/Ute

Source: German Language Society (Gesellschaft für deutsche Sprache e.V. – GfdS)

German Impact on the Arts

By Julie McDonald

Art & Design

German and German-American art has had a profound effect on the New World. Its practitioners have done everything from preserving vanishing wilderness and traditions to catapulting viewers into the challenges of futuristic designs. And what could be more American than prefabricated buildings and skyscrapers?

It was Walter Adolph Gropius (1883–1969) who designed many ultra-American rectangular towers with a skin of glass.

Gropius had advocated prefabricated construction before World War I. In 1919, he founded the Bauhaus School of Design by combining three schools of arts and crafts in Weimar, a city in Germany known for its culture. He moved the school to Dessau in 1925 and then resigned from the school in 1928 to return to private practice.

Gropius moved to England in 1934, became a professor of architecture at Harvard University in 1937, and chaired the Harvard School of Architecture from 1938 to 1952. He became a U.S. citizen in 1944.

In a distinguished career in Europe and the United States, Gropius brought an end to historically imitative architecture in favor of modern design. A purist, he believed both art and craftsmanship were fundamental to architecture.

Ludwig Mies van der Rohe (1886–1969) was director of the Bauhaus from 1930 until he closed it in 1933 rather than see Hitler shut it down. He came to the United States in 1937 and became head of the School of Architecture at the Armour Institute in Chicago. The school became the Illinois Institute of Technology, and he designed its campus.

Van der Rohe insisted "less is more." His functional designs include: the Seagram building in New York City; the glass-and-steel apartment buildings at 860 and 880 Lake Shore Drive in Chicago, now on the National Register of Historic Places; the Convention Hall in Chicago; the Cantor Drive-in Restaurant in Indianapolis; the Farnsworth House, a weekend retreat in Plano, Illinois; the Foster City apartments in San Mateo, California; the Museum of Art in Houston, Texas; the Public Library in Washington, D.C.; One Charles Center in Baltimore; and the Gallery of the Twentieth Century in Berlin.

Josef Albers (1888–1976) is noted for his geometric studies in color relationships. He taught at the Bauhaus from 1923 until 1933. He then headed the fine arts department at Black Mountain College in North Carolina for ten years and then was chairman of the Department of Arts at Yale University for ten years.

Emanuel Leutze (1816–1868), born in Germany and brought to the United States as a child, spent twenty years in Germany painting historical pictures, including the famous *Washington Crossing the Delaware.* He returned to the United States in 1859.

German-American artists created some of the most dramatic images of the American West, cowboys, and Indians, capturing on canvas a rapidly disappearing way of life. Among them were John Hauser (1859–1908), Charles Schreyvogel (1861–1912), Walter Ufer (1876–1936), who was a charter member of the Taos Society of Artists in New Mexico, and Fritz Reiss (1888–1953).

Americans recognize themselves in the paintings of Norman Rockwell (1894–1978), who was inspired by Joseph Leyendecker (1874–1951), the German-American artist who created the handsome Arrow Collar man for magazine advertisements in the first half of the twentieth century.

German-American painters included Charles Frederic Ulrich (1858–1908), who painted Pennsylvania Dutch scenes; William Ritschel (1864–1949) and Anton Otto Fischer (1882–1962), who did marine paintings; Jean Mannheim (1863–1945), a painter of California coastal scenes; and Franz Arthur Bischoff (1864–1929), who did impressionistic studies of California scenery.

Carl Rungius (1869–1959) portrayed big game animals in their habitats. Walt Kuhn (1877–1949) did clown paintings. Max Ernst (1891–1976) is remembered for his "anti-art" combination of objects in their natural state. George Grosz (1893–1959) created harsh images of war profiteers, and Adolph Dehn (1895–1968) created poetic landscapes and satires of art lovers.

Hans Hofmann (1880–1966) was a major abstract painter. Adolf "Ad" Reinhardt (1913–1967) and Franz Kline (1910–1962) were abstract Impressionists, a school of painters whose work reflected subjective emotions and responses of the artist to images not found in reality.

Daniel Garber (1880–1958) and Walter Emerson Baum (1884–1956) were members of the New Hope School of painting, a group of

Impressionists who sought to capture light and atmosphere in their works.

Emil Nolde (1867–1956) brought glowing color to Expressionism.

Max Kuehne (1880–1968) was a German-born painter influenced by the Impressionists, and Walter Koeniger (1881–1943) was known for his winter landscapes. Poor blacks were the subject of Julius Bloch (1888–1966), a social-realist painter.

Albert Bierstadt (1830–1902), the famous landscape painter of the Hudson River School, immortalized the American wilderness in two large canvasses for the nation's Capitol in Washington, D.C. Bierstadt's inspiration stemmed from an earlier era when Albrecht Altorfer (1480–1538), in his landscapes of the forest, expressed the Germans' mystic union with nature. His were the first German paintings that existed for the landscape itself.

The Artistic Legacy

The art movements Americans have embraced most enthusiastically have their roots in the German soul.

German art is Gothic, with ornamental line, complex composition, and an upward surge as opposed to the classic tradition of the Latins with its simplicity, regularity, and restraint.

The Gothic spirit created forms of unrest and suffering, and Germany was the only European country where the Gothic tradition remained pure through the Renaissance.

Germany's first contact with the Renaissance came in the personage of Albrecht Dürer (1471–1528). Durer started the vogue for the self-portrait and is responsible for the prominence of German drawings, engravings, and woodcuts. As a youth, he worked in the studio of Michael Wohlgemuth during the creation of *The Nuremberg Chronicle* of 1493, and woodcuts in this "account of the world to our time" have been attributed to him. This was the second book ever printed, following the Bible.

After the Germans recovered from the Thirty Years' War (1618–1648), the Gothic spirit became the Baroque, with curved forms and lavish ornamentation, and Rococo, with elaborate ornamentation combining shell work, scrolls, and foliage.

The architect Karl Friedrich Schinkel (1781–1841) gave Berlin its distinctive, classical grandeur with wide boulevards and buildings of heroic scale.

Romantic fairy tales and folklore subjects were favored by Moritz von Schwind (1804–1871), known as the "German Fra Angelico." Like the Italian painter, he filled his work with a spontaneous piety and gladness of spirit.

Both the Expressionists and the Surrealists (artists who find their images in dreams and the subconscious mind) claim Arnold Bocklin (1837–1901), whose work exhibited a vigorous naturalism. His best-known painting is *Self-Portrait with Death Playing the Violin.*

The first German exhibit of works by Vincent van Gogh, the Dutch artist, in 1905 inspired the founding of a group of artists who called themselves *Die Brucke* (The Bridge). They were more concerned with content than with form.

Next came *Der Blaue Reiter* (The Blue Rider) founded in Munich in 1910 by the Russian-born Wassily Kandinsky (1866–1944), who left Germany for Paris in 1934, and Franz Marc (1880–1916), who died at Verdun in World War I.

Ernst Ludwig Kirchner (1880–1938) was a painter of the modern city, and Erich Heckel (1883–1970) painted the sick and the dead. Austrian Oskar Kokoschka (1886–1980), who was also a poet and playwright, did portraits that signaled the imminent decay of the subjects.

Lyonel Feininger (1871–1956), the creator of airy cityscapes suffused with light, is among the artists recognized by most Americans, as are Swiss-born Paul Klee (1879–1940), who painted fantasy and enchantment and taught at the Bauhaus before leaving Germany in 1933, and Max Beckmann (1884–1950), known for monumental carnival figures and expressive lithographs.

When the Nazis denounced certain works of art as "degenerate," the famous Degenerate Art Show was mounted in Munich in 1937 before going on tour. The day after the opening, Max Beckmann went into exile. In 1939, Nazi propaganda minister Joseph Goebbels and other high-ranking party officials took the "degenerate" works they wanted from the exhibit and burned the rest in the yard of the Berlin Fire Brigade.

Otto Dix (1891–1969) practiced the New Objectivity, a severe and uncompromising realism. The Nazis also condemned his work as degenerate.

Kathe Kollwitz (1867–1945) is the most famous woman artist in the

German annals. Known for her drawings, woodcuts, and sculptures, her subjects were working people suffering from hunger, cold, poverty, and war. She created many lithographs and etchings of mothers and children. In 1919, she became the first woman elected to the Berlin Academy; the Nazis expelled her in 1933.

Paula Modersohn-Becker (1876–1907) painted mothers and children. Longing to have a child of her own, she died in childbirth.

Anselm Kiefer (1945–) is well-known in the United States. His emotional canvasses have been blasted by German art critics for reviving World War II memories that people want to forget. Huge, turbulent, and semi-abstract with heavy impasto, they evoke the ravages of war.

George Baselitz (1938–) was born in East Germany before moving to West Germany. He is a Neo-Expressionist, or postmodern. His career received a boost in the 1960s when a prosecutor seized two of his paintings because of their sexual overtones.

Gerhard Richter (1932–) was born in Dresden and has produced abstract and realistic works, as well as photographs and glass pieces. His work commands top dollar, with the painting of a square in Milan, Italy, bringing a record $37 million in a 2013 auction.

Literature

By Julie McDonald

German-American writers are seldom singled out in the United States, where they have been a fact of life since Franz Daniel Pastorius helped found Germantown, Pennsylvania, in 1683 and wrote the first primer schoolbook printed in Pennsylvania.

Pearl Buck (1892–1973) wrote about the Chinese, but her maiden name was Sydenstricker. Born in West Virginia, she grew up in China, where her parents were missionaries. Her novels and short stories include *A House Divided* and *The Good Earth.* She was awarded the Nobel Prize for Literature in 1938.

Theodore Dreiser (1871–1945) won acclaim for *Sister Carrie, An American Tragedy,* and *Jennie Gerhardt,* a novel about the German American experience.

Joyce Kilmer (1886–1918) is best known for his poem *Trees.* He wrote other poems and books and was killed in action in World War I. He was posthumously awarded the Croix de Guerre, a military medal from the French government.

Thomas Mann (1875–1955) fled Hitler's Germany to live in Switzerland, coming to the United States in 1938. He is known for his Joseph series, *Buddenbrooks* (a family name), and *The Magic Mountain*. The latter, set in a Swiss tuberculosis sanatorium, had a generation of American students worried about their lungs. Mann was awarded the Nobel Prize for Literature in 1929.

H.L. Mencken (1880–1956) was a German-American editor whose wit was as sharp as his pen. He wrote for *The Baltimore Sun* and was co-editor of *The Smart Set* and editor of *American Mercury*. His caustic writings jabbed at the middle class, organized religion, business, American culture, and what he called the Bible Belt.

Erich Maria Remarque (1898–1970) was born in Germany and served in the German army in World War I. He came to the United States in 1939, becoming a citizen in 1947. His powerful novel about those war experiences, *All Quiet on the Western Front,* is a classic. His second wife was Paulette Goddard, the film star.

Gertrude Stein (1874–1946) was a writer and art collector who lived on the Left Bank of Paris after 1903. Known as an innovative writer of novels and plays, she was an early adviser to writer Ernest Hemingway and a friend of artist Pablo Picasso. She wrote a best-selling memoir, *The Autobiography of Alice B. Toklas.*

John Steinbeck (1902–1968) was awarded the Nobel Prize for Literature in 1962. The best-known of his twenty-seven novels are *The Grapes of Wrath,* written in 1939, which depicts the plight of an Oklahoma farm family seeking a new life in California during the Great Depression; and *Of Mice and Men,* the tragic story of two migrant workers during the Depression.

Kurt Vonnegut Jr. (1922–2007), the son of third-generation German immigrants, wrote twelve novels known for their satire and mordant humor. He was a prisoner of war in Germany during World War II and survived the fire-bombing of Dresden, memorializing that experience in *Slaughterhouse-Five* and other writings. His novels include the ground-breaking *Cat's Cradle, Breakfast of Champions,* and *Jailbird.*

Fritz von Unruh (1885–1970), whose play *Bonaparte* in 1928 foretold the Hitler dictatorship, left Germany in 1932 for France and the United States. He did not return to his homeland for thirty years. His novels and poems stress the responsibility of the individual, as opposed to authoritarian societal models.

After 1933, a number of German writers left Germany for the United States. They included Stefan Zweig, Franz Werfel, Lion Feuchtwanger, and Thomas Mann's brother, Heinrich Mann, who wrote the novel that became the famous film, *The Blue Angel*, starring Marlene Dietrich. Paul Tillich and Reinhold Niebuhr, theologians known for their writings, also came to America.

The Literary Legacy

Some of the best-known themes of American literature are of German origin.

The Tristan and Isolde legend—of the fatal love affair between an Irish princess and the knight who escorts her to the king she is to marry—first appeared in 1210 in a poem by Gottfried von Strassburg. Parsifal, the perfect knight who devotes himself to heroic exploits, chivalrous love, serving God, and helping mankind, was born from the pen of Wolfram von Eschenbach in the same year.

Johann Wolfgang von Goethe (1749–1832) gave us an enduring version of Faust, the tale of a man who sells his soul to the devil in return for youth, knowledge, and magical powers. In the sixteenth century, the real Faust was Germany's foremost magician. As a child, Goethe was impressed by a puppet show about Faust, and his version of the story was published in 1833, the year after his death. The American musical *Damn Yankees*, which won the Tony award for best musical in 1955, is based on the Faust theme.

Most American children know and love the stories of *Hansel and Gretel, Rumpelstiltskin* and *Tom Thumb,* first put in writing by the Brothers Grimm, Jakob (1785–1863) and Wilhelm (1786–1859).

The earliest Germanic writing to survive is a translation of the Bible by Ulfilas (311–383), bishop of the Visigoths. Bible reading did not deter his parishioners from sacking Rome in 410.

In Germany, literature began in the time of Charlemagne (742–814). The great work of that early period was a harmony of the gospels. Soon after came Otfried's *Evangelienharmonic,* the first attempt in German poetry to replace alliteration with rhyme.

The interest in epic poetry extended to the old German sagas presented by wandering minstrels. The outstanding lyric poet of the Middle Ages was Walther von der Vogelweide (c. 1170–1228), who wrote love songs and poems. His poetry is still memorized today.

> *Who slays the lion*
> *Who slays the giant*
> *It is he who overcomes himself.*

Johannes Gutenberg (1398–1468) invented the printing process using movable type that survived, with little change, well into the twentieth century. He is credited with most of the work that went into printing the Latin Bible of 1456. It was the first book ever printed and brought the Bible and the printed word into lay hands for the first time.

The Reformation and Counter Reformation period brought *Epitolae obscurorum vivorum,* a satire by Johannes Reuchlin (1455–1522), supporting the struggle against the papacy. Martin Luther translated the Bible into German and achieved poetic quality in his church hymns. The defender of Catholicism was Thomas Murner, who wrote a satire, *Von dem grossen Lutherischen Narren (By the Great Lutheran Jester),* in 1522.

A notable literary work of the seventeenth century was the introduction of R. E. Raspe's *The Adventures of Baron Münchhausen* to the German public by Gottfried Burger (1747–1794), relating and expanding on the exploits of Baron Karl Friedrich von Münchhausen, who was famous for his tall tales.

Christoph Martin Wieland (1733–1813) published his classic novel, *Agathon,* in 1766. It was the beginning of the German psychological novel.

Johann Friedrich von Schiller (1759–1805), like Goethe, was inspired by the Greek ideal of human and artistic perfection. His *Don Carlos* showed his development as a dramatic poet, but his fame rests on plays written in his last years, *Wallenstein, Die Jungfrau von Orleans (The Maid of Orleans),* and *Wilhelm Tell (William Tell).*

E.T.A. Hoffmann (1776–1822) wrote stories of the supernatural and the fantastic, which became the basis of the opera, *The Tales of Hoffmann,* by Jacques Offenbach, and *The Nutcracker* ballet by Peter Ilich Tchaikovsky.

Charles Sealsfield (1793–1864) came to America in 1823, changing his name from Karl Postl. He wrote *The United States as They Are, in Their Political, Religious, and Social Bearings,* and fictional stories that entertained and helped lure German immigrants to Texas.

Heinrich Heine (1797–1856) was a creative genius of the nineteenth century who wrote poetry, prose, and literary criticism. Jewish and anti-Prussian, he immigrated to Paris in 1831. No German classical author is more widely read. The poetic cycle *Nordseebilder (North Sea Image)* is one of his works.

Rainer Maria Rilke (1875–1926) is well-known in the United States. His poetry, expressing love and the plight of man in search of positive, eternal values, has stood the test of time.

Hermann Hesse (1877–1962) wrote *Damian* and *Steppenwolf,* novels that indicted bourgeois society and were cherished by the American "flower children" of the 1960s. He was awarded the Nobel Prize for Literature in 1946.

Franz Kafka (1883–1924) was the most famous of the German literary Expressionists, writers who tried to grasp and write intuitively and find new modes of artistic expression. His best-known work is *The Metamorphosis,* a mesmerizing tale of a man turning into a cockroach. His other works include *Das Schloss (The Castle)* and *Amerika.*

Franz Werfel (1890–1945) wrote *The Song of Bernadette* (a nun's story that would become a Hollywood film) and *The Forty Days of Musa Dagh,* which also was well-known in the United States.

Heinrich Böll (1917–1985) received the Nobel Prize for Literature in 1972. The role of Catholicism in society was a major theme in his work. His books include *Gruppenbild mit Dame (Group Portrait with Lady)* and *Ansichten eines Clowns (A Clown's View).*

Günter Grass (1927–) wrote the famed novel, *The Tin Drum,* set before, during, and after World War II. It was the first of a trilogy set in Danzig, from which he fled after the war. He was awarded the Nobel Prize for Literature in 1999.

Other German winners of the Nobel Prize for Literature include historian Theodor Mommsen (1817–1903) in 1902; philosopher Rudolf Eucken (1846–1926) in 1908; writer, poet, and dramatist Paul von Heyse (1830–1914) in 1910; dramatist, poet, and novelist Gerhart Hauptmann (1862–1946) in 1912; and epic poet Carl Spitteler (1845–

1924) in 1918.

Carol Brown Janeway is the winner of the 2013 Friedrich Ulfers Prize for translating and publishing German books in English. The annual prize goes to a person "who has championed the advancement of German-language literature in the United States." The prize is awarded by the Deutsches Haus at New York University during Festival Neue Literatur, a weekend that features promising writers from Germany, Austria, and Switzerland.

Music

By Arthur Canter
The author is a professor emeritus of psychiatry at the University of Iowa in Iowa City. He writes and lectures about music and musicians.

The contribution made by German composers and musicians to the musical world in America and Europe is well-known.

Concert-goers have long known and loved Bach and Handel, Haydn, and Mozart, Beethoven, Brahms, and Wagner. If we add the rest of the Bach family, Bruch, Bruckner, Flotow, Hindemith, Humperdinck, Mahler, Mendelssohn, Offenbach, Reger, Schubert, Schumann, Richard Strauss, Webern, and Wolf, born in the nineteenth century, we have only touched a fraction of the German composers who left their mark on musical history.

Throughout the last two hundred years or more, the composers from Germany have dominated the style, form, and content of classical and popular music.

If we go back before the time of the Renaissance, we find that music was a vital part of the life of the German people. The peasants had their folk songs and folk dances, the burghers had town bands. They and the clergy had their church music and organists, and the nobility fostered the courtly musical activities.

The post-Renaissance period saw a flowering in the development of the German song, exemplified by the great Nuremberg Song Collection (1539–1556) of Georg Forster (c. 1510–1568).

The Reformation saw Martin Luther incorporate song in Christian worship, inspiring the chorale, which in turn became the basis of organ compositions and the cultivation of various kinds of church music.

To what can we ascribe the great numbers of German composers who appeared in the seventeenth and eighteenth centuries? Perhaps it was something in the spirit of the people that allowed musical talent and genius to be recognized and nurtured, as happened with Bach, Haydn, and Mozart.

In any event, the talent residing in the people was given outlets by the extensive patronage system that existed in Germany during the two-hundred-year period. Composers and musicians alike were supported by the three hundred states making up Germany. From these composers, and the musicians who played their music, came the development and refinement of all forms of musical expression, in particular the symphony, the quartet, and keyboard music.

The rise of German romantic poetry in the late eighteenth and early nineteenth centuries inspired a fresh blossoming of vocal melodies. It was natural that Romanticism in German literature be expressed in the music of German composers during the nineteenth century. Robert Schumann, Johannes Brahms, and Richard Wagner were particularly notable in this movement.

By the mid-nineteenth century, Germany was unquestionably in ascendency in the world of music. Coincidentally, this was the time when large numbers of Germans immigrated to America. The new immigrants brought with them a love of music, willingness to listen, to play, to sing, and to take instruction.

Thus, the first wave of German Americans provided the core of musical interest and activities in the major cities and towns of the United States, which attracted professional musicians to America when they faced troubled times in Germany.

A group of twenty-three young musicians, discontented with conditions in the revolutionary Germany of 1848, banded together in Berlin to form the Germania Society and immigrate to America. The Germania Society toured the United States for several years, providing cadres that helped spawn other orchestras across the country.

Many of these new orchestras were known as Germania Orchestras. They played the music of the great German composers and helped move those works into standard repertory.

Gottlieb Graupner (1767–1836), who came from Germany at the end of the eighteenth century, founded the Handel and Haydn Society in Boston in 1815. Carl Zerrahn (1826–1909) led the orchestra of this society, which developed into the Boston Symphony Orchestra.

In 1839, Charles Grobe (1817–1909) moved to the United States and became known for his "parlor music" compositions.

The Saxonia Band, introduced into America from Germany in 1848 and led by its organizer, Herman Kotzschmar (1829–1909), had its impact on the development of town band musical organizations and instruction in the playing of brass instruments. Kotzschmar was the first teacher of John Knowles Paine, who in 1875 became the first professor of music in the United States, at Harvard University.

The conductors of the newly formed symphony orchestras across America were for the most part German-trained in the traditions of Berlin, Leipzig, Munich, and Vienna. The ultimate in fine music during the latter half of the nineteenth century was considered to be written by ethnic German composers.

In 1871, Leopold Damrosch (1832–1885) came to New York City, where he founded the Oratoria Society and New York Symphony Society. He introduced German opera into the repertory of the newly founded Metropolitan Opera, which he directed. His son, Walter Damrosch (1862–1950), took over his post at the Metropolitan and directed the New York Philharmonic Society and the New York Symphony.

The German-American Theodore Thomas (1835–1905) played a prominent role in the development of several musical organizations across the United States, including the Brooklyn Philharmonic Society, which merged with the New York Symphony and later became the New York Philharmonic Orchestra. He helped organize the Cincinnati Musical College, which became the Cincinnati Conservatory. Thomas is best known for founding the Chicago Symphony Orchestra, which he developed out of his own Theodore Thomas Orchestra, a popular touring group in the style of the Germania orchestras.

Among noteworthy German-American conductors who have led major orchestras in the United States are George Henschel (1850–1934), the first director of the Boston Symphony Orchestra; Alfred Hertz (1872–1942), who conducted German opera at the Metropolitan for many years; Frederick Stock (1872–1942), who conducted the Chicago Symphony from 1905 until his death; Emil Oberhoffer (1867–1933), an organist in Minneapolis who helped found the Minneapolis Orchestra; Fritz Scheel (1852–1907), co-founder and first conductor of the Philadelphia Orchestra.

The list also includes Bruno Walter (nee Schlesinger) (1876–1962), the conductor of the New York Philharmonic and the CBS Orchestra, well-known interpreter of the music of Mahler; William Steinberg (nee Hans Wilhelm) (1899–1978), who directed both the Pittsburgh and Boston Symphony Orchestras and who, like Bruno Walter, fled Nazi Germany; Arthur Fiedler (1894–1979), the celebrated conductor of the Boston Pops Orchestra; Lucas Foss (nee Fuchs), the composer-conductor of many U.S. orchestras, including the Buffalo Philharmonic, who was a child refugee from Hitler's time.

Opera in America had its course influenced by German Americans. A German opera company was the first to occupy the then-new Metropolitan Opera House in the late 1800s. Many of the conductors of leading opera houses in the United States were ethnic Germans. Their numbers were increased by refugees from Nazi Germany in the 1930s.

Operetta and musical theater in America also were nurtured by composers of German origin. Victor Herbert (1859–1924), although born in Dublin, was half German and had trained in Stuttgart as a cellist. Edward Kuennecke (1888–1953) was known in the United States of the 1920s for his operetta *Caroline,* a resetting of his *Der Vetter aus Dingsda.*

Kurt Weill (1900–1950), a refugee from the Nazis, became well-known in America for his operettas and musical comedies based on jazz, blues, and cabaret music. These include *The Three Penny Opera, Lady in the Dark, Street Scene,* and *Mahogany.*

Frederick Loewe (1904–1988), who completed classical training in Germany before immigrating to the United States, is known for his work with Alan Jay Lerner on a number of Broadway hits such as *Brigadoon, Paint Your Wagon, My Fair Lady,* and *Camelot.*

Oscar Hammerstein (1846–1919) was an impresario who brought many fine singers to the United States. His grandson, Oscar Hammerstein II (1895–1960), a lyricist, collaborated with Rudolf Friml, Jerome Kern *(Showboat),* Vincent Youmans, and others on operettas and musicals. His most productive and longest-lasting collaboration was with Richard Rodgers. Together they created such Broadway hits as *Oklahoma!, Carousel, South Pacific, The King and I,* and *The Sound of Music.*

Hollywood film music also was influenced by German Americans. Paul Dessau (1894–1979) was a pioneer in composing background music for movies, opening opportunities for other composers such as Erich Korngold, Max Steiner, and Ernst Toch.

"Bix" Leo Bismarck Beiderbecke (1903–1931), the son of German immigrants, was a popular jazz cornet and piano player and composer in the 1920s. The city of Davenport, Iowa, his hometown, honors his legacy in an annual jazz festival held on the banks of the Mississippi River.

Sometime in the early 1900s, around the time of World War I and its aftermath, German influence upon the music of America passed its peak and has been slowly melding with the musical heritage of other cultures.

Stage and Screen

By Julie McDonald

When it comes to actors, Marlene Dietrich, affectionately called "the Kraut" by novelist Ernest Hemingway, is the magic name and face that comes to mind.

A Berliner with a laconic and languorous but electric manner, she didn't act. She sizzled. In her own inimitable style, she played everything from the sleazy cabaret girl in *The Blue Angel* to the dance-hall girl in *Destry Rides Again.*

"In her voice we hear the voice of the Lorelei," French novelist Jean Cocteau wrote of one of Hollywood's most famous actresses and a long-time fashion icon.

Marlene Dietrich introduced slacks to American women (for better or for worse), and she won the French Legion of Honor and the Medal of Freedom for making more than five hundred appearances before Allied troops during World War II. All of this was a long, fabulous journey for the daughter of a German army officer, who was born in 1901 and grew up as Maria Magdalene von Losch. She died in Paris in 1992 at the age of 90.

Other German-American actors who've made their mark in Hollywood include Horst Buchholz (1933–2003), who appeared in more than sixty films and played Chico in *The Magnificent Seven;* Heidi Klum (1973–), a supermodel and *Project Runway* reality show star; Romy Schneider (1938–1982), an icon in French cinema, remembered best for her 1970 film *Les Choses de la Vie (The Things of Life);* Claudia Schiffer (1970–), a supermodel and fitness guru who has starred in films, including *The Blackout* (1970); and Christoph Waltz (1946–), best known for his appearances in the Quentin Tarantino films *Inglourious Basterds* (2009) and *Django Unchained* (2012), for which he won Oscars.

A number of Germans have made their mark directing movies.

Ernest Lubitsch (1892–1947), one of the great film directors in American movie history, was born in Berlin and studied acting with Max Reinhardt, the noted German stage director. Lubitsch's earliest major features were made for Pola Negri, and he became the master of the film spectacle.

Lubitsch came to Hollywood in 1923 to direct Mary Pickford in *Rosita,* a picture that was never made. His films were noted for sophisticated and witty comedy. He directed *Lady Windermere's Fan* and *The Student Prince in Old Heidelberg* with Ramon Navarro, *To Be or Not to Be, Heaven Can Wait,* and others. He was the first to use songs as a part of the plot, in films starring Maurice Chevalier and Jeanette MacDonald.

Erich von Stroheim (1885–1957), son of a Prussian soldier, directed his first American picture, *Blind Husbands,* in 1918. He worked with Irving Thalberg at Universal Studios, and his talent for creating atmosphere was notable. His masterpiece, *Greed,* was severely cut by Thalberg, but it remains a powerful reflection of life.

Josef von Sternberg (1894–1959), another great director, was an American who hid his identify in a labyrinth of legend. Like Erich von Stroheim, he was of the tough, whip-and-jodhpurs school of directing. His first film was a disaster, but he found commercial success with *Underworld* in 1927, a preview of the gangster films of the 1930s. Von Sternberg directed Marlene Dietrich in *Morocco* (1930), *Dishonored* (1939), *Blonde Venus* (1932), and *The Devil is a Woman* (1935). His most famous work was *An American Tragedy* (1931). Paramount Studios separated von Sternberg and Dietrich in 1936, and the hot love affair between them also ended, which he said destroyed his talent.

Billy Wilder (1906–2002) was among the first of the film directors Hitler chased from Germany. From Vienna, he came to the United States in the 1930s. He made frothy pictures before moving on to the more substantial *Hold Back the Dawn* (1941), *Double Indemnity* (1943), and *The Lost Weekend* (1945). He also co-wrote and directed Gloria Swanson in *Sunset Boulevard* (1950). He returned to comedy with *The Seven Year Itch* (1955) and *Some Like It Hot* (1959). In all, he directed fourteen actors in Oscar-nominated performances.

Friedrich "Fritz" Lang (1890–1976), the German director Joseph Goebbels tried to recruit for the Nazi propaganda machine, came to America in 1934. He made *The Woman in the Window* (1944) with Edward G. Robinson and Joan Bennett, and *The Big Heat* (1953).

Other German refugees who directed films were Edgar Ulmer, *The Black Cat* (1934) and *Detour* (1945); John Brahm, who created Gothic films like *The Lodger* (1944); Douglas Sirk, *Thunder on the Hill* (1951); and Fred Zinnemann, *High Noon* (1952).

Carl Zuckmayer (1896–1977) wrote *The Devil's General* while in the United States. It was the first play to come to grips with the Nazi evil, and it was enthusiastically received in 1946 in post-war Germany.

Bertolt Brecht (1898–1956) left Germany in 1933 and, with composer Kurt Weill, created *The Three Penny Opera,* which ran for nearly a decade off-Broadway in the 1950s and 1960s. Other Brecht productions included *Mother Courage, The Good Woman of Setzuan,* and *Caucasian Chalk Circle.*

The German influence on motion pictures began with Athanasius Kircher (c. 1601–1680), a German Jesuit and mathematician in Rome. In 1640, he invented the magic lantern, a device for projecting images. Early in the nineteenth century, Baron Franz von Uchatius (1811–1881), an Austrian artilleryman, used a zoetrope, an instrument for creating illusions with a series of hand-drawn pictures, to demonstrate the performance of a cannon ball. Some of the earliest film strips included footage of Kaiser Wilhelm reviewing his troops.

The earliest German theater was religious drama, which survives in the famous *Passion Play,* performed every ten years at Oberammergau, and which has been transplanted to the Black Hills of South Dakota and other venues throughout the world. Mel Gibson in 2004 made the movie, *The Passion of Christ,* which used the *Passion Play* as its center. Few German plays are produced in the United States because of the language barrier and because German drama is heavier and more intellectual than the fare favored by most modern audiences.

Opera is the best-loved German performing art, a taste that influences all other forms of public presentations. Ballet exists as an adjunct to the numerous opera houses. Companies in Stuttgart and Düsseldorf have achieved a distinctive style and repertoire.

Folk Art and Collectibles

By Dianne Stevens

From barns to birth certificates, from farm machinery to tombstones, German Americans have enhanced everyday objects with extraordinary art.

Metal hinges were shaped as tulips, guns were carved and inlaid with brass and copper, and barns were decorated with colorful hex signs. Today, such folk art abounds in many states.

German-American folk art is characterized by bright colors and simple motifs borrowed from religion, nature, and myth. The lily of the field design, often called a tulip, and the tree of life motifs are both religious symbols. The *distelfink* is the legendary bird of good luck. A unicorn harks back to medieval legend as the guardian of maidenhood. The thistle represents hard work and perseverance. Lovebirds represent love, marriage, and romance.

In Pennsylvania Dutch country, *fraktur,* hex signs, painted furniture, and redware pottery are created to this day.

Fraktur

Fraktur is a striking combination of text in *fraktur* lettering—an angular, sixteenth-century Gothic typeface—and design rooted in the medieval art of manuscript illumination. A revival of the art began in the mid-eighteenth century at the Ephrata Cloister and spread to the rest of Pennsylvania, Maryland, and Virginia.

Originally drawn on parchment or paper with a finely cut tail feather from a crow or pheasant, using India or drawing ink, *fraktur* mixed words and vivid watercolors. Fanciful symbols were borrowed from nature (birds, tulips), design (hearts), religion (angels, devils), and mythology (mermaids, unicorns).

Many *fraktur* artists were ministers in Lutheran or Reformed churches or schoolmasters in church schools. Children were taught the art in school. *Fraktur* became so popular that in the mid-nineteenth century it was preprinted.

Fraktur was a personal art to the owners because it decorated items like baptismal records, confirmation records, marriage and death certificates, house blessings, hymns, inscription pages on gift books, Bibles, church records, birthday greetings, and school awards. Since it was private and tucked away in Bibles and books or pasted onto blanket chest lids, *fraktur* was an acceptable art form to sects like the Mennonites and Amish that frowned on public art.

Today, handmade eighteenth- and nineteenth-century *fraktur* is one of the most sought-after Pennsylvania Dutch arts, sometimes worth thousands of dollars. Artists still practice the art and offer custom pieces at reasonable prices.

More than one hundred sixty examples of *fraktur* are in the collection of the Henry Francis du Pont Winterthur Museum in Winterthur, Delaware. The examples include Valentines, marriage records, birth and baptismal records, and pictures ranging from floral to abstract.

Hex Signs

The colorful hex signs on many Pennsylvania German barns are not designed to scare away witches. They are purely decorative, their flower and geometric designs meant to be cheery and welcoming.

The painting of hex signs began in the southeastern corner of the state between 1830 and 1850. Ivan Hoyt, who painted many hex signs, speculates the signs appeared when manufactured paint pigments were available and farmers mixed those with sour milk as a binder.

The first signs were geometric designs in red, black, and yellow. Blue was seldom used since imported indigo was expensive. Farmers painted their own signs until the early 1900s when traveling barn painters picked up the art.

Some of the same hex designs seen on barns appear on Bibles, with designs similar to early Christian symbols. Some popular hex sign symbols include tulips, representing faith; pomegranates, long life and fertility; hearts; and the *distelfink*. The scalloped border represents either smooth sailing or a life of ups and downs, Hoyt says.

Nutcrackers

Nutcrackers, a popular German woodcraft, were originally carved as functional devices in the early 1700s to crack nuts but have since become popular collectibles.

The Leavenworth Nutcracker Museum in Leavenworth, Washington, has more than six thousand nutcrackers on display, including a bronze Roman nutcracker dated between 200 BC and AD 200. It was found in 1960 after being buried for more than eighteen hundred years.

Joan Liffring-Zug Bourret photo

Nutcracker museum sign, Leavenworth, Washington

The U.S. Postal Service in October 2008 issued four Nutcracker stamps featuring nutcrackers designed by Virginia artist Glenn Crider.

The stern nutcrackers usually are caricatures of authority figures, so there is a bit of irony in having kings, policemen, military officers, and noblemen put to work for anybody with a nut to crack.

Bauernmalerei

Bauernmalerei, similar to Norwegian rosemaling, is a German folk art that decorates furniture, clocks, woodwork, and plates with painted designs.

Characterized by cheerfully colored designs on dark backgrounds, *Bauernmalerei* uses heraldic, geometric, and floral motifs. The rose is a favorite subject, followed by the tulip, daisy, poppy, violet, and other garden flowers painted in simple or artistic arrangements.

German Americans painted all types of furniture. A popular piece was a dower chest used to store a new bride's quilts and blankets. The German Biedermeier style of furniture, popular among German professional classes, also was painted with warm landscape scenes and sometimes amusing scenes.

Redware

Redware is a reddish brown, earthenware pottery often decorated with yellow, green, black, and blue. Colonists brought the first redware to New England, Virginia, and the Chesapeake Bay area. But it was German-speaking immigrants who made the most elaborate pottery.

The three basic types of redware were undecorated, slip-trailed, and sgraffito.

Slip-trailed redware was created by drizzling a thin clay slip through a quill for lettering and design. Sgraffito was made by brushing the surface of damp clay with white or yellow liquid slip and using a stylus to make designs. The most elaborate sgraffito and slip-trailed redware were made in Pennsylvania and used as gifts. The undecorated redware was used as everyday dishes.

By the mid-nineteenth century, redware lost popularity as stoneware, glass, tin, and china became readily available. The folk art is enjoying a revival today and is again available from potters. Antique redware pieces command high prices in the collectible market.

Beer Steins

Beer steins originated in Germany in the late 1400s when hordes of flies invaded central Europe in the summer and the Black Death still lingered in people's memories. Because most beer was consumed in outdoor gardens, beer drinkers decided to put lids, equipped with a thumb lift, on their drinking mugs to keep out the flies.

Most early steins were made of wood or porous earthenware because pewter, silver, and glass were too expensive. Eventually, stoneware was developed, an excellent material for steins. Renaissance artists lavishly decorated the steins with scenes from historical, allegorical, and biblical tales. Shapes varied from conical to melon to a ram's horn shape.

Villeroy and Boch began creating steins in 1836 in Mettlach. They used Renaissance designs in brightly colored clays and glazes and enjoyed what was known as the golden age of Mettlach steins from 1880 until 1910. The company's trademark, the village's Old Abbey Tower, is on the bottom of most genuine Mettlach steins, which can sell for thousands of dollars today.

Hummels

A young nun from southern Bavaria was the creative genius behind the Hummel figurines, a popular collectible.

In 1927, at age 18, Bertha Hummel began studies at the Munich Academy of Fine Arts. She befriended two fellow students who were nuns, and, through this friendship, her interest in religious life blossomed.

In 1931, she began her novitiate as a Franciscan nun at the Convent of Siessen in Bad Saulgau, Germany, continuing her studies as Sister Maria Innocentia. Her charming sketches were made into cards that caught the eye of the enterprising German porcelain manufacturer, Franz Goebel.

He gave Sister Maria Innocentia and the Convent of Siessen final artistic control over each figurine and promised the nun's signature would be on the base of each piece. Since Sister Maria's death in 1946 at age 37, which many think was brought about by the privations of World War II—the Nazis did not like her art—the Convent has supervised the Hummel art.

Hummel figurines first appeared in 1935 and are known for their muted colors, soft glazing, and precious features. Authentic Hummels all have the M.I. Hummel signature on their base. Today, the Hummel line has expanded to plates, prints, calendars, Nativity sets, plaques, bells, and lamps, though Goebel's company quit manufacturing the figurines in 2008. A collection of more than a thousand rare Hummels can be seen in Rosemont, Illinois, at the Donald E. Stephens Museum of Hummels. Stephens was the first mayor of Rosemont and began collecting the figurines in the 1960s after a trip to Europe. He gave the collection to the city in 1984, and the museum opened to the public in 2011.

Cuckoo Clocks

The cuckoo clock hasn't changed that much over the centuries. Why mess with something that's so perfectly goofy and fun?

A cuckoo clock takes note of the hour with a little bird that pops out of a door and calls "cuckoo." Sometimes the bird will flap its wings, sometimes its call will be accompanied by music. Most of the clocks are shaped like chalets and are hung on a wall.

The first description of a cuckoo clock, owned by an Augsburg aristocrat named August von Sachsen, came in 1629. The clock's inventor is unknown, but the Black Forest—in what is now southwestern Germany—became known for producing the clocks by the mid-1700s.

Modern cuckoo clocks were developed in Switzerland in the late 1800s. The clocks are now made in three chalet styles—Black Forest, Bavarian, and Swiss. Many of the clocks play *The Happy Wanderer* or *Edelweiss* (which is not an Austrian folk song but a song Rodgers and Hammerstein wrote for "The Sound of Music" in 1959). Clockmakers sometimes replace the cuckoo bird with animals, dancers, or beer drinkers.

The world's largest collection of cuckoo clocks is at the Cuckooland Museum in Cheshire, England. Two other notable collections are in museums in Gütenbach and Fürtwangen in the Black Forest region of Germany.

Quilts

Unlike *fraktur* and painted furniture, Germans did not bring quilting as a folk art with them to the United States. They borrowed it from their American neighbors and stitched their own identity into their quilts.

The Amish have created some of the most treasured quilts. Living in the world, but not of it, the Amish separated themselves from outside influences, giving their quilts distinct characteristics. The Amish use large fields of dark but vibrant fabrics stitched into bold patterns with as many as twenty stitches to an inch. The colors of their quilts reflect their own dress, for they wear deep, rich tones under their dark cloaks. In the past twenty years, quilting has enjoyed a bit of a resurgence, moving from a rural-based social art to more sophisticated and artistic free-form designs.

German Folk Music

The Germans sailed for America with music in their souls and their instruments in their luggage.

The Hinrichs' family, for example, provided the music for the ship on which they sailed, receiving a reduced fare for their passage. They came in the 1860s to escape German military conscription and settled along the Mississippi River at Clinton, Iowa.

During the American Civil War, German immigrant soldiers on both sides sang in the camps, sometimes within earshot of each other.

When they weren't singing, German Americans formed bands with brass, accordions, and the concertina. When a farmer built a barn, the loft was used for dances. The floor was polished, and neighbors and relatives brought cakes and sandwiches to feed the dancers. Music was furnished by the sons of neighbors, all of whom were of German extraction.

Music notes were often written down as the young listened to their parents singing around the supper table. Mothers often sang and yodeled as they did their daily household chores. Thus much of the music was German folk music with an American adaptation—polkas, waltzes, Laendler, and Schottische. Thus the polkas of Germany, Poland, and what is now the Czech Republic were intermingled.

Harold Loeffelmacher of New Ulm, Minnesota, founded his Six Fat

Dutchmen band in 1936 and toured widely with never fewer than eleven players—all on the slender side and none of them of total German ancestry. At one time, twenty-one polka bands were from New Ulm.

One of the more famous German band leaders was Lawrence Welk, who was born in a German speaking community, Strasburg, North Dakota, in 1903. He later participated in local midwest bands and then went on to direct bands in North Dakota and eastern South Dakota.

Too shy at first to introduce songs because of his heavy German accent, Welk and his accent went on to fame with his nationally televised "champagne music" shows—with lots of polkas and waltzes. The shows live on in reruns even today.

German Folk Costumes

By Karin Gottier

When Americans seek to go back to their roots, they often reach for the colorful clothes of their immigrant ancestors as a quick and visible symbol of ethnic affiliation.

Native dress has its historical roots in rural communities of the seventeenth century and later. At first dictated by the local authorities, clothing styles changed slowly over the decades. Native dress evolved in highly structured, conforming village societies that demanded total integration of the wearer into the group.

In most European countries at the turn of the century, there was a trend toward the creation of a "national" dress. It was intended for those who were not part of rural society but who wanted to show their national affiliation.

Young Germans adapted the traditional dress forms of the Alpine areas, and the *dirndl* dress was born. The *dirndl* was comfortable and becoming, it was easy to care for, and, for its wearers, it epitomized the simple, wholesome country life.

Because the *dirndl* dress is not native dress but folklore fashion, it is subject to fashion changes, and it spawned a whole fashion industry. It can be a jumper-blouse-apron combination, a two-piece dress with apron, or even a one-piece dress with apron. In each case, it always has a full skirt and an apron. The hemline may rise or fall, the color palette

146—

may change, certain details may be emphasized (depending on which native dress inspired the designers), but it always has the unmistakable look of ethnic clothing. A *dirndl* dress is usually worn with white, or sometimes colored, lace-knit knee socks, buckled shoes, and jewelry based on traditional pieces.

Native dress prescribes exactly who wears what, when, and how, and what colors and combinations of accessories are appropriate on a given occasion, according to the wearer's age and marital status. *Dirndl* dresses place no such restriction on the wearer. Each woman can choose the style her taste and pocketbook allow.

Although little girls sometimes wear a wreath with their *dirndl* dresses, floral wreaths with ribbons—proper for certain Ukrainian and Polish costumes—are not customary with German folk dress.

None of the traditional German costumes use floral wreaths of that type, although tall, crown-like structures of artificial flowers and tinsel are worn by brides, bridesmaids, and young women walking in religious processions. The wreath has traditionally been a symbol of maidenhood, and married women consider it inappropriate to put wreaths on their heads.

Color choice is individual when choosing *dirndl* fashions. However, one never sees the national colors featured. To wear one's flag is considered in poor taste.

Women adapted the *dirndl* dress in the pre-World War I period, while men gave up their stiff collars and tight vests for the short leather pant—the *lederhosen*—that originally was a traditional garment of the Alpine lumber worker. Shortened from knee-length to mid-thigh, it became a comfortable and durable item of clothing for hiking and leisure activities. Many a man cherishes the by-now shiny and greasy *lederhosen* of his youth. These days, *lederhosen* are back again to being close to knee length, reflecting modern preference for longer shorts for men.

Since those early days, the *dirndl* dress and the *lederhosen* have become, for German Americans, the means of identifying with their roots. The *dirndl* is usually a jumper with a low-cut bodice, in bright colors, featuring bands of elaborate embroidery on the skirt and bodice. Blouse and apron are typically trimmed with lace, lace inserts, and ornamental braiding. The bodice is decorated with buttons or chains. The outfits are readily available in catalogs and online from stores specializing in

German imports and gift items.

Although any German-American festival is an opportunity to see *dirndl* fashions in all their variety, it is the dance groups that illustrate the multitude of traditional costumes, with Bavarian-style predominant. Characteristic are the bodices laced with silver chains and hooks. The full-flying skirts, fringed shawls, and aprons are as familiar as the *lederhosen*, green vests, embroidered suspenders, and green hats of the men.

Even though *lederhosen* have become symbolic of German costume, they are actually worn in only a very small area of Bavaria. Much more common are the *kniebundhosen* or knickers. The pants were universally worn until the French Revolution when they were replaced by long pants. Made of dark or yellow leather, knickers are worn by the men in many dance groups in America, together with a colored vest, either solid or striped, depending on the region the group represents.

Other dance groups appear in costumes from North Germany and Friesland and wear wooden shoes. Wooden shoes are indigenous in all of Germany, varying in form from region to region. The men wear blue-and-white-striped shirts, bell-bottomed sailor pants, and fishermen's caps. The women wear neat, brocaded bonnets with long, embroidered ribbons, long skirts, fitted jackets, aprons, and embroidered shawls. Men in the Hessian groups wear fur caps and blue smocks. The women favor embroidered, knitted shoulder scarfs and embroidered stockings.

The folk dance groups of displaced Germans—from Hungary, Transylvania, Czechoslovakia, and Yugoslavia—are most conscious of their native dress. The most spectacular of these folk costumes come from the Transylvanian-Saxons and Danube-Swabians.

Because of their settlement history, the Transylvanian-Saxons' costumes retain many medieval elements. They feature lavish embroidery of colored satin stitch and black-and-white cross-stitch. Aprons, blouses, and headscarves are creations of sheerest gossamer tulle embroidered in white or black, contrasting in their airiness with the heavy silver belts, huge ornamental chest pins, and the jeweled hairpins of the married women. The men appear in high black boots, pants, white shirts embroidered in black cross-stitch, velvet ties with colored floral embroidery showing the initials of the wearer and the date the tie was made. In winter, both men and women wear heavy, white sheepskin coats, fur side in, that have been profusely trimmed with colored embroidery and leather applique.

The Danube-Swabian women stand out with their large, bell-shaped, pleated skirts, either white or in floral patterns, worn over layers of starched white petticoats. Their shoulder scarfs are masterpieces of colored embroidery on black, with lavish widths of hand-knotted fringe. The shawl is artfully draped in a neat pattern across the wearer's back and pinned into place to give it the proper shape. Aprons are often black and trimmed with soutache (a flat braid) or lace. They appear rather stiff and shield-like without many gathers at the waist. The girls and women usually wear their hair in braids wrapped around the head, set off by a black velvet ribbon.

The Danube-Swabian costume for men is rather dark: black trousers tucked into black boots, black vests with silver buttons, white shirts, and black hats. The men and women wear a sprig of rosemary pinned to their clothes, as was customary for special festivals and dances.

Although the costumes worn by German-American dance groups and by others are as diverse as the places their ancestors came from, the universal *dirndl* fashion, together with *lederhosen,* have become the favored costume.

The American Federation of German Folk Dance Groups maintains a list of folk dance groups on its website: germanfolkdancers.org

History of German Folk Dance

By Karin Gottier

All over the United States, in cities and towns, German dance groups, both large and small, cultivate the dances of all regions of Germany.

Some groups are sponsored by German-American societies, and some are international folk dancers who have formed performance ensembles. Some are made up of German language students in high school or college. Others simply dance recreationally for the social interaction and to learn more about German culture.

Members of these groups range in age from children to senior citizens. Some are native-born Germans, some are of German descent, and many aren't German at all. What unites them is the joy of dancing and the determination to preserve the German heritage.

The seeds of the contemporary folk dance movement were planted in the early decades of the twentieth century. Folk dance pioneers, who had come into contact with the English and Scandinavian folk dance movements, began to comb the countryside, notating and collecting the dances they found. Inspired by the idealism of the youth movement, they perceived a need to provide activities for young adults that promoted physical and emotional well-being and that also fostered a sense of community.

Because of these early contacts with Britain and Scandinavia, many English and Swedish dances have become a permanent part of the German folk dance repertoire. From these early days, too, date the *Jugend und Gemeinschaftstänze* (youth and community dances). These were dances in the folk idiom, created by dance leaders to appeal to young people. Several of these dances have become folk dances and are beloved by German and American folk dancers alike.

In the United States, the German folk dance scene is as diverse as in Europe.

The most visible groups are the Bavarian Schuhplattl clubs, which hold dance competitions, encourage the correct wearing of Bavarian costumes, publish a newsletter, and hold national and international conferences.

Other dance groups have been founded by the displaced Germans from Silesia, Pomerania, East and West Prussia, Romania, Slovakia, the Sudeten and Egerland (now in the Czech Republic), and Hungary. These groups wear their costumes, sing their songs, and dance their dances as a link with a homeland that is no longer theirs and to pass along their cultural heritage to their children.

German folk dancing, as well as German music, dialect, costumes, and customs, can be divided into two areas—the mountainous, predominantly Catholic South, and the flat, predominantly Protestant North.

The Alpine culture of the South extends across national borders into Austria and, in some cases, into Alemannic Switzerland.

Dances of the mountain areas fall into several categories:
- The traditional social dances of one or two figures.
- The turning-couple dances such as the *Ländler*—a smooth, stepped dance in 3/4 time in which dancers continuously intertwine their arms in intricate positions.
- The *Dreher*, which uses pivot steps in 2/4 time.
- The *Zwiefacher*, which alternates in irregular sequences be-

tween waltz and pivot steps.

The show-off dancing so unique to the Alpine area, the *Schuhplattler,* a vigorous men's dance consisting of various stomps and slaps, appears to have been described in the thirteenth century in the poetry of Neidhart von Reuental, a *Minnesinger* (troubadour). While in its pure form it is danced spontaneously and freestyle, it experienced its greatest development with the establishment of organizations dedicated to the preservation of the Alpine dance, costume, and custom during the last decades of the nineteenth century.

Because of the demands made by group performance, uniform slapping patterns were developed within Schuhplattler clubs. Today, a *Schuhplattler* is made up of the following parts: The entry march; the actual Plattler, in which the men show off with stomping and slapping while the women spin in place or travel around the circle; the chase, in which the men stalk their partners; and finally, after the men catch their partners, the waltz.

Another major group of dances is ritual in nature and is tied to specific seasons, festivals, and customs. They are always group dances, very often men's dances. Included in this group are the dances of the various guilds. One of the most famous examples is the *Schäffletranz* of Munich's coopers guild (for wine and beer makers). The various sword dances, such as the *Unterwössner* and *Überlinger* sword dance, can be classed in this category as well.

The dance traditions of North Germany are mostly survivals of eighteenth and nineteenth century ballroom dances. Here we find quadrilles, long-way sets—variously called Anglaise, Ecossaise, or Francaise, according to their formation—as well as couple dances. There is also a greater variety of steps. Waltz, polka, mazurka, and schottische steps, as well as step-hops, step-swings, skipping, and running steps all appear in North German dances. These dances require larger areas and move somewhat more quickly than the dances of Southern Germany.

Few ritual dances are still performed in the northern areas even though at one time these, too, were practiced. In 1747, Anton Veithen described a sword dance performed by men decorated with bells and ribbons, which culminated in the interlocking of the swords and lifting of the leader over the men's heads. The sword dance tradition is common in all of Europe and the British Isles.

Holidays, Religion, and Diversions

By Julie McDonald

Christmas

Most ingredients of "an old-fashioned American Christmas" actually come from Germany: Santa Claus (St. Nicholas), *The Messiah* by George Frederick Handel, and the Christmas tree, to name a few.

One of the most enchanting German Christmas traditions is St. Nicholas. The patron saint of sailors and students, St. Nicholas has been venerated in Germany since the twelfth century. St. Nicholas statues stand guard in towns along the Rhine, and churches bear his name.

St. Nicholas was a fourth century Bishop of Myra in Asia Minor, revered for his generosity and worshipped by sailors for miracles at sea and in harbor. He also helped poor girls by providing their dowries. Stockings, hung by the fire to dry, were miraculously filled with gold so the girls could marry.

St. Nicholas is said to have brought back to life three children who had been murdered and stored as pickled meat in the house of a wicked butcher. The children carried out church duties thereafter and were rewarded with small gifts on December 6.

The custom of a gift-giver representing a bishop took root, and the question, "Have you been good?" preceded the presentation. St. Nicholas was accompanied by a dark figure wrapped in old clothes or fur who carried the sack of presents and dealt with bad children. He was called Knecht Ruprecht (Black Santa).

Famed cartoonist Thomas Nast (1840–1902), who came to the United States from Germany as a child, created the white-bearded Santa Claus with a pack on his back, combining St. Nicholas and Knecht Ruprecht. Nast's Santa, introduced during the American Civil War, also was a self-portrait—as round and cheery as the artist who created him.

The Christmas carol *Silent Night* was composed on Christmas Eve in 1818 by Franz Gruber, the son of an Austrian linen weaver. From 1816 to 1829, Gruber was soloist and organist at the Catholic Church in Oberndorf near Salzburg. The words to the carol were written by the priest, the Rev. Josef Mohr.

For many Americans, the Christmas season truly arrives with the performance of *The Messiah,* the oratorio composed in twenty-four days in 1741 by George Frederick Handel. Even though the premiere of the work was in April 1742, the arias concerning the birth of Christ have linked the oratorio to Christmas. *The Messiah* was written long after Handel became a British subject, but the country of his birth was Germany.

Christmas Trees, Ornaments

The origin of the Christmas tree is hidden in the mists of the past, but we do know we must give up the pleasant image of Martin Luther and his family in front of a candle-lit tree. The combination of the festive evergreen and lights didn't happen that soon.

The tradition of creating a Christmas pyramid of pine boughs and decorations, and later of decorating an entire tree, started in Germany, with guilds decorating trees as early as 1570. A 1605 manuscript in Strasbourg described "fire trees with roses cut from multicolored paper, apples, cakes, tinsel, and sugar hanging from the branches."

The trees were common in urban homes in Germany by the early 1700s. In 1798, Duchess Elisabeth Charlotte of Orleans wrote a letter to her daughter describing "box bushes on tables with a candle fixed to every branch. This looks absolutely charming."

Placing a star at the top of the tree became a common practice in the last half of the eighteenth century.

German settlers introduced the Christmas tree in America, but its wide popularity came after England's Prince Albert (who had been born in Germany) installed one in the royal palace in 1841, and magazines began to feature beautifully decorated trees.

The earliest record of a Christmas tree in the United States is found in the diary of Matthew Zahm, who wrote about his family going into the woods to cut the tree on December 20, 1821. An 1825 issue of the *Philadelphia Saturday Evening Post* described "trees visible through the windows, whose green boughs are laden with fruits richer than the golden apples of the Hesperides."

In some parts of Germany, trees were decorated with edibles: apples, nuts, and raisins. Fancy cookie molds were brought at Christmas to make Matzebaum, almond cakes with raised images. Most were eaten when the tree came down, but some were put away and used year after year. After slow-baking at a low temperature, Matzebaum were painted with homemade vegetable dyes and dated. Thicker shapes made from almond-flavored dough were called marzipan. Miniature fruits and vegetables were favorite shapes for these sweets, popular in Germany since the Middle Ages.

Another decorating favorite was the white Springerle made from egg dough seasoned with anise seeds. The finest Springerle molds were made by woodcarvers. Other treasures from the homeland were cookie cutters made by tinsmiths in the shape of the moon, stars, hearts, trees, and flowers.

In Pennsylvania Dutch country, white cookies were sprinkled with red sugar "for pretty," and a washbasketful of cookies was not enough for Christmas. Included were *Christbäume* (pretzel-shaped to represent praying hands) and paper-thin sand tarts.

The Pennsylvania Dutch also set out baskets on Christmas Eve for the Christ child to fill with cookies, candies, nuts, and raisins. The baskets were made of rye straw to represent the manger and lined with a clean white napkin to symbolize the swaddling clothes of Jesus.

Around 1880, the glassmakers in the German state of Thuringia discovered a new method of blowing glass bells, balls, and animals, and silver-coating the inside.

In 1900, a merchant named Woolworth brought the first colorful glass-ball ornaments, called Kugels, to the United States. The Kugels lasted season after season and became a traditional ornament. Tinsel strips to hang on the branches became popular, and angel's hair, spangles, and silver stars were made from glass fiber.

Some of the loveliest ornaments ever created were the small, silver- and gold-embossed cardboard Dresden Christmas tree ornaments. Remarkably detailed, they were shaped like dogs, cats, suns, moons, frogs, turtles, exotic animals, sea life, bicycles, skates, cars, boats, pianos, and other musical instruments. Other German ornaments were made from shiny wire twisted and tied into stars, butterflies, and rosettes. Germany contributed the custom of the Putz, a fence-enclosed scene of figures and toys or a Nativity scene beneath the tree.

The Germans always have unveiled the Christmas tree on Christmas Eve in a theatrical moment of sudden radiance. German Americans, however, were more likely to put up the tree sooner and enjoy its beauty longer.

Germans were in the forefront of Christmas tree stand design. In 1877, Johannes Eckardt of Stuttgart applied for an American patent for a revolving musical tree stand. Four more men with German names received patents for their stands, and in 1899, Alfred Wagner of St. Louis patented a stand that held water for the tree and that rotated the tree with an electric motor.

Those who could not afford the metal stands put their Christmas trees in buckets of coal. The poor farmers of Pennsylvania got double use from each tree, removing the dry needles and, for the next year, making a "snow tree" by covering the bare branches with cotton.

Christmas morning among the Moravians of Pennsylvania has always had a special flavor. Each home had a corner set aside for a Nativity scene. People went to the woods in September to dig moss; they tended it carefully in the cellar until it became the green grass of the Christmas Putz. Frequently, a winding road was built of sawdust or sand to accommodate several hundred small wooden animals making their way to Noah's ark.

In contrast to the simple and devout celebration of Christmas, "General" Johann August Sutter, the flamboyant German whose California land was the center of the Gold Rush, lavishly celebrated December 25, 1847, just before his property was overrun by gold-crazed prospectors. The menu that day at the Rancheria de Hoch included soup, salmon, pigs' feet and pepper, frijoles and beef, veal, and all manner of game, with champagne and wine. Music and dancing went on until dawn.

Through every age and political circumstance, the Germans have celebrated Christmas. The United States, a young nation yearning for the glow of tradition, embraced the German customs.

Christmas Pyramids

By Helen Kraus

If your ancestors were from Germany, the word "pyramids" would conjure up Egypt as well as visions of wooden pyramids brought out at Christmas.

The tree that is associated with Christmas was banned in many German provinces because it was considered a waste to cut down a tree merely for ornamentation. In part of Alsace, an ordinance stated that no person "shall have for Christmas more than one bush of more than eight shoe lengths." In 1531, that meant a tree or bush that was less than four feet tall.

In many other provinces, cutting down a tree without permission could mean a fine or imprisonment. Because of those realities, plus the fact the church considered the Christmas tree a form of pagan worship, people looked for new ideas.

In Saxony, men would fashion leftover wood into little fences. These would surround wooden animals, often sheep with wool batting glued to their sides, presenting a pastoral scene and reminding the pious Saxons of the shepherds who were told of Christ's birth. In a crib or manger scene in Bavaria, religious cards would represent the holy family. In all provinces, the wooden pyramid, made of materials such as wood, paper, or tin, came into use as a "Christmas tree."

Paddles on the apex of the pyramid were propelled by a steady current of warm air rising from candles placed under and somewhat to the sides of the paddles. At first, the paddles were made from paper and had a small circular piece of paper connected to them. Paper angels hung from those circles. When the heat from the candles made the paddle turn, it looked as though the angels were flying above the Christ Child's crib.

Since paper burned easily, tin was substituted, and then wood. Because tin and wood were more substantial than paper, the pyramids grew in height—two, three, four, and even five stories tall. All were connected to, and turned with, the same center dowel that was turned by the paddles.

Candles are used with pyramids because they are symbolic of Christ, the "Light of the World" to Christians. Because wax candles were expensive, candles of tallow were used, or the candles were lit for only a short time. The pyramids were, and still are, often decorated with pine boughs, and often the pyramid is painted a deep green so that any bare spots are not so noticeable.

Some people call the pyramids "windmills."

The largest Christmas pyramid stands in the Christkindl Market in Dresden, Germany. It is 45 feet tall, with five rotating levels and life-sized wooden figures.

This enormous outdoor pyramid stands during the Christmas season in Fredericksburg, Texas.

Cooking the German Way

By Mary Sharp

Anneliese Heider Tisdale of Cedar Rapids, Iowa, is known for her excellent German cooking—and for her memoir of growing up in Munich, Germany, during World War II. Anneliese, a longtime teacher of languages, has lived in the United States since 1947. She became a U.S. citizen in 1952. Her mother was an excellent cook, but Anneliese says she didn't know a thing about cooking when she arrived in Iowa as a G.I. bride. She watched her mother-in-law in the kitchen and bought a cookbook. "I figured if I could read, I could cook."

One of Anneliese's proudest possessions is her mother's cookbook, written in Old German Script and published in 1936, complete with a drawing of a pine branch by eight-year-old Anneliese. The recipes in the cookbook list ingredients in grams and liters and also have charming—though non-specific—measurements such as "a little salt," "a little milk," and "baking powder to cover the tip of a knife." Anneliese still has her mother's kitchen scale with the wooden block holding various weights. She also has her own kitchen scale and, when her three children started asking for their favorite German family recipes, she weighed ingredients and converted them into English measurements of cups and teaspoons.

In the process, she says, she cut some of the butter and cream from those traditional recipes—retaining the flavor, but cutting calories and fat. "You keep the bacon, but you render it, and throw away the grease," she says, recalling times during and after the war when bacon grease was a prized commodity and no one would ever have discarded it. In another concession to healthier eating, she says, turkey has replaced the traditional goose on many a German Christmas dinner table. Anneliese includes some of her family recipes in her memoir—*Christmas Trees Lit the Sky*—and also agreed to share some of those recipes in this book. (The *"Christmas Trees"* in her memoir's title refer to the red and green flares Allied planes dropped over German cities at night to mark target areas.)

The "new" German cooking—just like that in other countries—is lighter and more varied, though people can still find traditional fare. Many of the quality German restaurants, Anneliese notes, have much longer menus than American restaurants, offering venison, wild boar, escargot, fresh trout, and duck. A *Gasthaus* will offer more traditional fare—sausages, sauerbraten, *Schweinshaxn* (pork knuckle), schnitzel, and dumplings—along with many and varied beers. Anneliese notes that eleven restaurants in Germany earned three-star ratings from the famed Michelin Restaurant Guide in 2015. She adds that Bavaria, Germany's largest state, and its capital, Munich, are great places to taste the new *deutsche Küche.*

Anneliese was eleven years old and living in Munich when World War II began. She learned English from her German-American cousin, whose family had lived in New York City for ten years.

After the war, Anneliese served as an interpreter for the Allied occupation forces in Munich. After immigrating to the U.S. and marrying, she had three children, earned a college degree, and taught languages in the public schools in Cedar Rapids, Iowa, for almost thirty years. Now retired, Anneliese lives in Cedar Rapids and enjoys reading from her memoir in midwestern book stores. She is working on a sequel about her life in the United States. Her memoir is available from Author-House.com, Amazon.com, Barnes & Noble, and from local booksellers.

The cooking that German immigrants brought to the United States in the 1800s, she notes, was traditional fare.

"The German kitchen, *deutsche Küche,* basically offered hearty food—dumplings, potatoes, heavy breads—because it fed farming people who were working hard," she says.

The desserts were elegant—cakes, cookies, and tortes (many-layered cakes with fillings).

Anneliese says her children's favorite German recipes include liver dumpling soup—"they don't like liver, but they love liver dumpling soup!"—pancake soup, *Rindsrouladen* (beef roll-ups), potato salad mixed with cucumber salad, kohlrabi "fixed the way my mother fixed it," radish sandwiches, *Gesundheitskuchen* (Health Cakes), and *Lebkuchen* (Gingerbread).

One of the elements of German life she misses is the Sunday afternoon *Spaziergang* (Walk), where people would stop at a café for coffee and for a pastry chosen from a vast array of baked goods behind a long, glass counter.

On the rare occasion her parents would splurge and stop for *Kännchen Kaffee,* "I remember it was so difficult as a child to choose" from all the pastries. "You received a little coupon to take to the table, and then you handed the coupon to the waitress so she could bring you the delectable pastry you'd chosen."

The adults would order a little pot of coffee—about 2-1/2 cups. There were no free refills. The coffee pot "usually arrived on a little silver tray with a tiny pitcher of cream and a tiny plate of paper-wrapped sugar cubes."

Although Anneliese has perfected many German recipes over the years, she still misses the hearty breads so readily available in Germany, plus the *Brötchen* (hard rolls), *Bretzen* (big pretzels), *Weisswurst* (white sausage with flakes of parsley), *Kalbsnierenbraten* (veal roast wrapped around veal kidneys), and her mother's *gespickter Lendenbraten* (beef filet larded with bacon pieces).

She also fondly remembers the huge chestnut trees with their large white or lilac blooms that are such an integral part of a Bavarian beer garden.

"Many families would bring their lunches, and buy a beer, and have their lunch in the beer gardens," she says. "We used to gather the chestnuts and take them out in the woods to the deer-feeding stations and watch the deer feed. When I see the deer outside my windows here in Iowa, I think of that."

German-style Food in America

By Joan Liffring-Zug Bourret

By the millions, Americans flock to German- or Bavarian-style restaurants in leading tourist sites and cities. One reason: They'll never leave hungry. If there is a sign featuring Bavaria or Germany at a restaurant, you have arrived at a table of abundance.

On the menu you are likely to find sauerkraut and red cabbage, sausages, bratwurst, pork, and beer, followed by an interesting choice of tortes and cakes. Any German-style celebration, virtually anywhere in America or Germany, means beer and sausages and plenty to eat.

The pencil-thin, high-fashion image does not usually depict German men as well as women.

German-style cooking is found in every Amish or Mennonite community in Pennsylvania, Ohio, Missouri, Indiana, Illinois, Iowa, and Kansas, with restaurants serving the foods of these plain people.

In the Pennsylvania Dutch country of Lancaster County in southeastern Pennsylvania, the people's closeness to the soil is evident in the bounty of produce seen at roadside stands. The production, preparation, and preservation of food play a main part in setting the pace of life.

Recipes reflecting German heritage are handed down from generation to generation. These "hand-me-downs" are typically served family style at tables laden with soup, main dishes, side dishes of vegetables, sweets and sours, noodles, and salads. Sweets, like pudding or cake, are sometimes served before the main meal because there may not be room after the hearty feast.

The Amish themselves usually do not own and operate restaurants, though the more liberal Mennonites run the restaurants and the tourist industry featuring Amish foods. Amish women, however, may cook in the restaurants. Some communities offer tours that offer the opportunity to eat in an Amish or Mennonite country home.

In Kalona, Iowa, Amish-Mennonite dinners usually include different kinds of tapioca puddings. In Pennsylvania Amish-Mennonite restaurants, pickled-red-beet eggs are a treat, and shoo-fly pie is a traditional dessert.

People come to Frankenmuth, Michigan, for the famous chicken dinners. In New Braunfels, Texas, the local specialty is smoked turkey—a native American bird advertised with a Tex-German accent.

German restaurants in Fredericksburg, Texas, offer a variety of choices that may include sausages such as bratwurst and bockwurst made with veal, pork, and traditional spices, or a dinner of schnitzel Holstein (breaded veal cutlet topped with poached eggs, gravy, and anchovies).

Lovers of Tex-Mex food have a German—William Gebhardt—to thank for the perfect combination of spices, with extracted and ground pulp from the chili pod, that gives their favorite dishes the right taste.

Born in Germany, Gebhardt came to the United States and opened a café in 1892 in the back of Miller's Saloon in New Braunfels, Texas. He soon discovered that the German community loved chili but couldn't make it until home-grown chili peppers were in season. In 1894, he developed the first commercial chili powder by running pepper bits through a small home meat grinder. Two years later, Gebhardt and Albert Kronkosky opened a factory in San Antonio for the production of chili powder. The factory continues to produce chili powder today.

The Amana Colonies of Iowa are famous for their German-style foods served family style. The meals feature Amana hams and beef and full bowls of side dishes which may include applesauce and cabbage. Each restaurant in the Amanas has its own version of rhubarb pie, and it is a treat to compare the double crust, single crust, meringue-topped, and many other taste delights, particularly during the fresh rhubarb season. In season, the rhubarb also is used to make *Piestengel,* a favorite wine.

From Iowa, Missouri, Wisconsin, Texas, and other states where many Germans settled, meat markets ship products stressing the traditions of Germany. The Texans ship smoked turkeys as well as the traditional bacons, hams, and sausages. Among the products available from Pennsylvania and Ohio are their specialties: pretzels, jellies, and jams.

Many German immigrants founded breweries, especially in Wisconsin and Missouri. Oktoberfests nationwide feature beer and bratwurst. The Wurstfest in New Braunfels, Texas, in October draws thousands of tourists. Beer, brats, and other German foods also appeal to the thousands of people attending Milwaukee's summer weekend German Fest.

Those are just a few of the joyous celebrations of German heritage, with all the traditional fare, you can find throughout the United States.

Restaurant sign, Leavenworth, Washington

Recipes

Appetizers and Soups

German meals often start with a soup, with appetizers reserved for more formal meals.

Caraway Cheese Sticks
Käsestangen Mamas

Anneliese Heider Tisdale, Cedar Rapids, Iowa

My piano teacher, Herr Kammermeier, ate lots of these and drank plenty of my mother's *Johannisbeerlikör* when he was invited—much to my consternation—to our house once a year. He used to pull my hair above my ear if I had not practiced the piano as much as he thought I should.

1 cup flour
1-1/2 cups grated
    Emmenthaler cheese*
7 tablespoons butter

1 egg yolk, lightly beaten with
    1 teaspoon water
Caraway seeds

Preheat oven to 350°. Blend flour, cheese, and butter in food processor or by hand. Chill. On pastry cloth, roll out dough to a thickness of about 1/4-inch. Cut into strips about 4-1/2 inches long and 1/2-inch wide. Brush with beaten egg yolk and sprinkle with caraway seeds. Bake on ungreased baking sheet until golden, about 10 to 12 minutes.

Note: You may substitute any freshly grated hard cheese such as Asiago or Parmesan.

D. H.

Cheese Grater

Sausage Balls
Wurstbällchen

1 pound mild sausage
1 cup sharp Cheddar cheese

2 cups Bisquick® mix
2 tablespoons water

Preheat oven to 400°. Spray baking dish or rimmed cookie sheet. Mix together ingredients. Roll mixture into balls about 1-inch in diameter. Place balls in baking dish or on rimmed cookie sheet. Bake 10 minutes. Drain on paper towels.

Ham Roll-Ups
Schinken Rollups

8 ounces thinly sliced cooked
   ham
1 (8-ounce) package cream cheese

2 tablespoons mustard
1 teaspoon Worcestershire sauce

Mix softened cream cheese, mustard, and Worcestershire sauce. Spread thin layer of mixture on slices of ham. Roll each slice into a "log." Refrigerate for at least 2 hours. Cut into 1-inch sections. Lay each piece on its side so the design shows.

King Ludwig's Restaurant sign
Leavenworth, Washington
The restaurant takes its name from a famous
German King Ludwig II.

Mama's Goulash
Gulasch

Anneliese Heider Tisdale, Cedar Rapids, Iowa

1-1/2 pounds lean stew meat
2 tablespoons vegetable oil
2 medium chopped onions
1 clove crushed garlic
1 tablespoon paprika
3/4 teaspoon caraway seed
1 tablespoon tomato paste
2 cups beef broth

Salt and freshly ground
    black pepper to taste
1 to 2 tablespoons flour
Water
Freshly minced parsley (optional)

Brown meat in hot oil in skillet or Dutch oven. Remove meat and set aside. Add onion and garlic to the pan drippings and cook a few minutes on low setting. Add paprika and caraway seed and stir to blend. Add tomato paste, beef broth, salt, and pepper. Return meat to pan.

Cover and cook over low heat, stirring often, until meat is tender, about 1-1/2 hours. Mix the flour with some water to make a smooth paste and add to the meat mixture, stirring to keep smooth. Cook a few minutes until gravy thickens. Taste to see if you want to add more seasonings. Serve over wide noodles or hot boiled potatoes. Serves 4 to 5.

E. F.

Garlic Cloves

Cream of Wheat® Dumpling Soup
Grießnockerlsuppe

Anneliese Heider Tisdale, Cedar Rapids, Iowa

1 cup milk
2 tablespoons butter
3/4 teaspoon salt
6 tablespoons Cream of Wheat®
1 lightly beaten egg

Chopped parsley to taste
Pinch of nutmeg
4 cups chicken broth
Chopped chives

Bring milk to a boil. Add butter and salt. While stirring, add the Cream of Wheat®. Continue stirring, over low heat until the mass pulls away from the side of the pan and forms a ball. Cool about 10 minutes. Add the egg, parsley, and nutmeg. Let stand for 20 minutes. Bring chicken broth to a boil. Use 2 teaspoons to form small *Nockerl*—oblong-shaped dumplings (or little round ones). Drop dumplings into boiling broth. Simmer for 10 minutes. Sprinkle with chopped chives (or parsley) and serve. Serves 6 to 8.

Pancake Soup
Pfannkuchensuppe

Anneliese Heider Tisdale, Cedar Rapids, Iowa

Whenever we had leftover pancakes, my mother made pancake soup.

Cold, thin pancakes
Chicken broth

Chopped chives

Roll up cold pancakes and cut into thin strips, like noodles. Store in refrigerator. When ready to serve, put the pancake strips into individual soup bowls, pour hot chicken broth over the pancake strips and sprinkle with chopped chives. Serve immediately.

Note: See Basic Pancake recipe. Thick American-style pancakes won't work for this soup.

Beef Goulash
Rindergulasch

This soup's flavor improves if made a day ahead.

2 pounds lean beef,
   cut into 1/2-inch cubes
1/4 cup vegetable oil
1-1/2 cups chopped onion
2 cloves crushed garlic
1 teaspoon paprika
1/2 teaspoon salt

3 peeled and cubed potatoes
1 (6-ounce) can tomato paste
1 teaspoon sugar
1 teaspoon caraway seed
1/2 diced green pepper
Salt and pepper to taste

In large pot, brown meat in hot oil. Remove meat and add onion, garlic, paprika, and salt. Sauté until onions are soft. Return meat to pot. Add 1 quart water until meat is tender, about 1-1/2 hours. Add remaining ingredients and cook another 30 minutes. Add more water if necessary. Salt and pepper to taste. Serves 8.

Note: This recipe works well in a slow cooker, but brown meat mixture on stove before putting in the slow cooker to cook.

D. H.

Sliced Onion

Liver Dumpling Soup
Leberknödelsuppe

Anneliese Heider Tisdale, Cedar Rapids, Iowa

Dumplings:
1 package stale rolls
1-1/2 cups warm milk
1/2 pound beef liver
1 finely chopped onion
1/2 cup chopped fresh parsley
2 eggs
2 teaspoons dried marjoram

Dash garlic salt
Grated rind of 1/2 lemon
1 teaspoon salt
1/2 teaspoon pepper

Soup:
Beef broth, canned or homemade
Chopped chives for garnish

Cut rolls into thin slices. Place in large bowl and pour the warm milk over the bread. Cover and let soak about 30 to 40 minutes. Prepare liver by removing membrane and then finely chopping. Set aside. Sauté onion in butter. Add the liver, onion, and rest of ingredients to the bread and milk mixture. Mix well.

If the mixture is too soft, add some bread crumbs. Bring a large pan of salted water to a boil. Dip your hands in a bowl of cold water and form dumplings. Gently lower dumplings into the boiling water. Simmer for about 20 to 25 minutes. In separate pan, bring beef broth to a boil. Put a dumpling into each soup plate and ladle hot beef broth over it. Sprinkle with chopped chives. Serve immediately.

Note: I like using Earth Grain® French rolls for this recipe.

D. H.

Soup and Bread

Potato Soup
Kartoffelsuppe

4 cups diced potatoes
1/2 cup diced onion
1/2 cup diced celery
1-1/2 cups water
2 cups milk

1 carton (8 ounce) sour cream
  with chives
1 tablespoon flour
2 chicken bouillon cubes
Salt and pepper to taste

Wash, peel, and dice potatoes. Dice onion and celery. In saucepan, combine potatoes, onion, and celery. Cover with water and cook until tender, about 20 minutes. Add 1 cup of milk and heat. In small mixing bowl, combine sour cream and flour. Blend remaining cup of milk with sour cream mixture. Pour over potatoes in saucepan. Add bouillon cubes, salt and pepper. Heat while stirring until soup thickens.

Note: Diced ham can be added to this recipe.

Apple-Onion Soup
Apfel-Zwiebelsuppe

1 pound thinly sliced onions
1/4 cup butter
1 large (49-ounce) can
  chicken broth
2 beef bouillon cubes

1-1/2 cups hot water
1 can frozen apple
  juice concentrate
2 cups apple juice
1 pinch pepper, to taste

Dissolve beef bouillon cubes in 1-1/2 cups hot water. Cook onion in butter in large saucepan over medium heat until onion is soft, but not brown (about 10 minutes). Add beef bouillon, chicken broth, apple juice concentrate, and apple juice. Bring to a boil, then cover and reduce heat to medium-low. Simmer for one hour. Soup can be served over sliced raw onions, with a slice of green apple on top.

Cheddar Cheese Chowder

2 cups water
2 cups diced potatoes
1/2 cup sliced carrots
1/2 cup sliced celery
1/4 cup diced onion
Salt and pepper to taste
1 cup diced cooked ham

2 cups shredded Cheddar cheese

Sauce:
2 cups milk
1/4 cup butter or margarine
1/4 cup flour

In a saucepan, cover vegetables with water and cook until tender. Drain and cool. In a separate saucepan, blend milk, butter, and flour. Heat while stirring until thickened. Add vegetables. Simmer for 30 minutes, stirring to prevent burning. Add ham and cheese. Simmer until cheese melts and ham is heated through.

Caraway Beef Stew
Kümmel Rindergulasch

3 tablespoons vegetable oil
1 minced clove of garlic
2 medium chopped onions
2 pounds beef stew meat
Salt and pepper to taste
2 tablespoons caraway seed

6 cups beef broth
1/2 teaspoon cinnamon
3 large potatoes, peeled and
    cut in 1-inch cubes
3 large carrots, peeled and
    cut in 1-inch chunks

Heat oil in large saucepan on top of stove. Add chopped garlic and onions and cook until soft and translucent but not brown. Stir in beef, salt, and pepper, and brown. Pour extra oil off beef and discard. Stir in caraway seeds and cook for about a minute. Add beef broth and cinnamon, and bring to a boil. Reduce heat to medium-low and simmer until meat is tender, about one hour. Stir in potatoes and carrots. Cook until tender, about 30 minutes. When done, stew can be thickened, if desired, by mixing together 1 tablespoon of flour and 1/4 cup of water and then stirring into stew. Simmer about five minutes.

Leek and Potato Soup
Lauchsuppe

Anneliese Heider Tisdale, Cedar Rapids, Iowa

This was my grandson's favorite soup when he was a college student and staying with us.

3 cups leeks
4 cups potatoes
3 tablespoons butter
1/4 cup chopped parsley
1 clove of minced garlic
  (optional)
2 quarts chicken broth

1/2 cup cream (I use fat-free
  Half & Half)
Salt and freshly ground pepper
  to taste
3 tablespoons chopped parsley or
  chives, for garnish

Wash leeks and drain well. Slice thinly the white and light green parts of the leeks, discarding the top, dark-green part. Peel potatoes and cut into small cubes. Melt butter in saucepan and sauté the potatoes and leeks in the butter for about 10 minutes; do not brown. Add the parsley and the garlic and sauté a few minutes more. Add the chicken broth and simmer for about 45 minutes, until the vegetables are tender. You can mash some of the soup with a potato masher, or leave it as is. Stir in the cream (or Half & Half) and add salt and pepper to taste. Do not boil. Ladle into individual soup bowls (in Germany, we used soup plates) and garnish with chives or parsley.

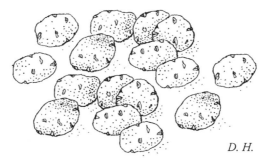

D. H.

Potatoes

Breads, Pancakes, and Dumplings

Bread has been a part of German meals since recorded history. The loaves tend to be smaller and denser than American breads. Traditional German breads include *Graubrot* and *Kommisbrot* (rye), *Mischbrot* (wheat and rye), *Bauernbrot* (wheat), *Vollkornbrot* (whole-meal), and *Schwarzbrot* and pumpernickel (dark rye).

The heavier, dark, whole-grain breads, such as pumpernickel, are more prevalent in Northern Germany. The lighter, more finely ground wheat breads prevail in Southern Germany. A number of bakeries specialize in German breads and offer them in retail shops and to online shoppers.

Farmer Bread (Sourdough)
Bauernbrot

1-1/2 packs yeast
1 quart warm water
2 tablespoons sugar
4 cups white flour
***

8 cups white rye flour
4 cups white flour
2 tablespoons salt
1 teaspoon sugar
2 cups warm water

Crumble yeast into a large bowl. Mix with warm water and sugar. Slowly add 4 cups flour, mixing well until smooth. Cover with a clean cloth and let sit for 24 hours at room temperature. This is your sourdough starter. After 24 hours, stir again, cover, and let stand another 24 hours. In a large bowl, stir together the rye flour, 4 cups of white flour, salt, and sugar. Gradually stir in the sourdough starter, alternating with 2 cups of warm water (adding a little at a time). Turn out dough onto clean, floured surface and knead thoroughly for 15 minutes, until dough is smooth. Place dough in large bowl, cover, and let rise until doubled (1 to 2 hours). Punch down dough, remove from bowl, and knead again for about five minutes. Shape into two loaves. Place on baking sheets, cover, and let rise for an hour. Preheat oven to 400 degrees. Bake 45 minutes or until done. Cool on rack.

Streusel Coffee Cake
Streusel Kaffeekuchen

3/4 cup sugar
1/4 cup shortening
1 egg
1/2 cup milk
1-1/2 cups flour
2 teaspoons baking powder
1/2 teaspoon salt

Streusel filling/topping:
1/2 cup firmly packed
   brown sugar
2 tablespoons flour
2 teaspoons cinnamon
1/2 cup chopped walnuts
2 tablespoons melted butter

Preheat oven to 375°. Grease and flour 9x9-inch pan. In mixing bowl, mix together sugar, shortening, egg, and milk. Sift together flour, baking powder, and salt. Add to sugar mixture. Mix well. Spread half the batter into pan. Sprinkle half the sugar-nut mixture on top of that. Add remaining batter to pan. Sprinkle rest of sugar-nut mixture on top. Bake 30 minutes.

E. F.

Black Walnuts

Grandma's Pretzels
Omas Brezel

1 package active dry yeast	4-1/2 cups flour
1/2 teaspoon sugar	1 beaten egg
1-1/2 cups warm beer	Coarse salt

In large mixing bowl, dissolve yeast and sugar in warm beer. Add flour and blend well. Turn dough onto lightly floured surface. Knead 8 to 10 minutes until dough is smooth and elastic. Place dough in greased bowl, turning to grease the top. Cover and let rise in a warm place about one hour or double in size. Preheat oven to 475°.

Cut dough into 24 pieces. Roll each piece into a ball. With floured hands, roll each piece between palms to form a rope 14 to 16 inches long. Twist into a pretzel shape. Cut in half. Place on greased baking sheets about 1-1/2 inches apart. Brush each pretzel with egg and sprinkle with coarse salt. Bake 12 to 15 minutes until golden brown. Cool on wire rack. Serve warm. Makes 2 dozen.

Notes: For one *Neujahrspretzel*, use about one-third of the dough to make a longer, thicker pretzel that will take up a full baking sheet. Cross the ends to form a circle. Bake 15 to 17 minutes in 475° oven. For many Germans, baking such an oversized pretzel is a New Year's Day tradition. Two people pick up the baked pretzel by a side and tug—whoever gets the bigger piece will have the greater good fortune in the year ahead.

D. H.

Grandma's Mixing Bowl

Fruit Jens
Faugens

Doris Andresen, Nevada, Iowa

1 quart milk, warmed
1 cake yeast (or 1 envelope
  dry yeast)
5 eggs
1 teaspoon salt
1/2 teaspoon vanilla (or
  cardamom)

3/4 cup sugar
10 cups flour
Raisins or currants (optional)
Frying oil (or Crisco®)
Powdered sugar

Heat milk to lukewarm. In small bowl, dissolve yeast in small amount of the milk. In large bowl, beat eggs well. Add warm milk, sugar, salt, and vanilla. Gradually mix in 5 cups of flour. Add yeast mixture and mix. Add rest of flour until dough is sticky. Add raisins or currants, if desired.

    Shape dough in a round ball, cover, and let rise in warm place until "bubbly" and almost double in size. Stir down, cover, and let rise again. Heat frying oil to boiling. Drop dough by spoonsful into oil. Interesting shapes will result and will roll over when brown on one side. Remove with a slotted spoon. Roll in powdered sugar.

Notes: "My mother would serve these on Christmas Eve. On Christmas morning, she would warm them for breakfast in a double boiler and shake powdered sugar over them again. I now pop them in the microwave for a few seconds."

E. F.

Raisins and Grapes

German Fritters
Deutsche Faugens

1 package yeast	6 eggs
3/4 cup lukewarm water	1 teaspoon salt
1 cup flour	1/2 cup sugar
2 cups milk	1 teaspoon cardamom
1 stick butter or margarine	1 cup raisins
1 cup flour	1 lemon

In mixing bowl, dissolve yeast in lukewarm water. Add flour and beat well. Cover and let rise. In saucepan, heat milk and butter. Bring to a boil and pour in flour. Mix and remove from heat. Cool to lukewarm, until mixture leaves the sides of the pan. Then add eggs, salt, sugar, cardamom, and raisins. Mix well. Add juice of 1 lemon. Grate lemon rind and add. Mix well. Cover and let dough rise until it is light. Heat oil in skillet. Drop dough by tablespoons into hot fat and turn when brown. Remove and drain. Roll in sugar while still warm.

D. H.

Basket of Eggs

Salads and Fruits

In Germany, salads, or *salate,* are typically served on the same plate as the main dish and vegetable. Some salads can be a meal all by themselves.

Bavarian Potato Salad
Bayrischer Kartoffelsalat

Anneliese Heider Tisdale, Cedar Rapids, Iowa

6 to 8 firm white waxy potatoes
    (not baking potatoes)
1/4 cup finely chopped
    onion or green onion
3 tablespoons vegetable oil

1 cup water
1 chicken bouillon cube
1/4 cup white wine vinegar
Salt and pepper to taste
Freshly chopped chives

Wash potatoes and cook in their skin. Peel while still warm. Cut potatoes into thin slices and place in large bowl. Add onion and sprinkle with oil. In large measuring cup, mix water, bouillon cube, and vinegar and heat until warm. Pour over potatoes. Add salt, pepper, and chives. Gently mix. (You can mix potato salad with cucumber salad or endive salad at this point; recipes for both salads are included in this section.) Adjust seasonings to taste. Let stand for 30 minutes before serving. Sprinkle more chives on top.

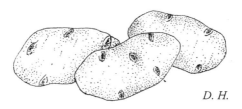

D. H.

Potatoes

Beet Salad
Rote Rübensalat

Anneliese Heider Tisdale, Cedar Rapids, Iowa

3 to 4 red beets
2 tablespoons vinegar
1 teaspoon salt

Dressing:
1/4 cup water
1/4 cup vinegar
2 tablespoons sugar
1 teaspoon caraway seeds
2 tablespoons chopped onion

Put beets in pan with enough water to cover. Add vinegar and salt. Boil until beets are tender. Peel the beets while still warm. Slice beets. Prepare dressing and pour over sliced beets.

Note: This tastes best if salad is allowed to marinate at least 8 hours or overnight.

Ham and Apple Salad
Wurstsalat

Anneliese Heider Tisdale, Cedar Rapids, Iowa

3/4 pound ham, cut in strips
1/3 pound good bologna
(not the ring style)
2 cups mayonnaise
6 teaspoons of half and half
(I use fat-free)
1 cup thinly sliced small
gherkin pickles

1 cup finely chopped onions
3/4 to 1 teaspoon dill weed
1 teaspoon sugar
1 tablespoon capers or to taste
3 chopped, hard-boiled eggs
(optional)
2 to 3 red-skinned apples

Prepare meats. Mix mayonnaise with half and half, gherkins, onion, dill weed, sugar, and capers. Fold in eggs, if used. Dice apples, leaving on skins, and add. Let stand 8 hours or overnight.

Note: We served this with crusty hard rolls or crusty bread sticks, but rye bread or crackers work well, too.

Ham Salad
Schinkensalat

4 cups diced cooked ham
2 cups water

1 cup vinegar
1 finely chopped onion

Combine all ingredients in a non-metal container, or porcelain crock or bowl. Cover and refrigerate overnight.

Herring Salad
Heringsalat

Anneliese Heider Tisdale, Cedar Rapids, Iowa

1 large tart apple
1 (16-ounce) can diced beets
1 finely chopped medium onion
2 diced dill pickles
1 pound herring in wine sauce

1 tablespoon chopped capers
Dill weed, fresh or dried, to taste
1 cup mayonnaise or
    more to taste

Peel, core, and chop apple. Drain beets. Drain and coarsely chop herring. Combine all the ingredients, adding the mayonnaise last. Refrigerate 1 day. Stir well and adjust seasoning, if necessary, before serving.

Notes: This salad must be made at least one day ahead for the flavors to blend. It does not taste that good when first made. Serve with crusty hard rolls or crusty bread sticks, cocktail rye bread or crackers.

E. F.

Beets

Cucumber Salad
Gurkensalat

Anneliese Heider Tisdale, Cedar Rapids, Iowa

2 cucumbers
Salt to taste
2-1/2 tablespoons vinegar
Pepper to taste
Pinch of sugar
1 tablespoon chopped onion

optional
1/2 teaspoon fresh chopped
dill weed
(or 1/4 teaspoon dried)
Fresh chopped chives

Peel and slice cucumbers into bowl and sprinkle with salt. Let stand for 15 minutes. Drain off some of the liquid if necessary. Add the rest of the ingredients and serve.

Note: This can be added to Bavarian potato salad. (See recipe in this section.)

Curly Endive Salad
Endiviensalat

Anneliese Heider Tisdale, Cedar Rapids, Iowa

1 head curly endive greens
2 to 3 tablespoons vegetable oil
Salt to taste

2 to 3 tablespoons vinegar
or lemon juice

Wash endive leaves several times. Discard dark outer leaves. Cut leaves crosswise (like noodles). Put in lukewarm water for 30 minutes. Drain well. Pour the dressing over salad. Adjust seasoning if necessary.

Note: We like this salad best when it is mixed with the Bavarian potato salad. (See recipe in this section.)

Tomato Salad
Tomatensalat

Anneliese Heider Tisdale, Cedar Rapids, Iowa

4 sliced tomatoes
2 tablespoons chopped onions or
  green onions
Chopped chives

Dressing:
1/2 cup vegetable oil
3 tablespoons vinegar
3/4 teaspoon salt
Pinch of sugar

Arrange the sliced tomatoes in a bowl. Sprinkle with chopped onions. Pour the dressing over all. Sprinkle with chives. This salad is better if allowed to marinate for an hour or two.

Ronneburg Cottage Cheese
Hüttenkäse

Ronneburg Restaurant, Amana, Iowa

1 (16-ounce) carton cottage
  cheese
1 chopped green onion,
  including tops

2 tablespoons buttermilk
1/4 teaspoon salt
Dash of pepper

Combine all ingredients. Refrigerate. Serves 4.

Note: You can increase the amount of chopped onion, depending on taste.

D. H.

Tomato

Cold Schwabian Potato Salad
Schwäbischer Kartoffelsalat

Connie Lauzon, Mount Angel, Oregon

3 pounds yellow Finn potatoes
    (or fingerling potatoes)
1/2 pound finely chopped onions

Dressing:
1/2 cup cider vinegar
1/2 cup vegetable oil
1-1/2 teaspoon salt
3/4 teaspoon seasoned pepper

Wash potatoes well. Put potatoes in kettle and cover with salted water. Boil until fork can be inserted with just a bit of pressure. Drain and let cool in refrigerator. When well-cooled, peel and slice very thinly, about 1/8-inch thick. Very finely chop the onion and add to potatoes. In a cup, combine cider vinegar, oil, salt, and pepper. Mix well, Pour over potatoes and toss. Keep refrigerated. Taste improves with time and will be good up to a week after preparation. Serves 10.

Notes: There is nothing in this recipe to make one sick so it can be left out at picnics. Yellow Finn potatoes can't always be found, so use potatoes that are not baking potatoes and will hold their shape after cooking, like red potatoes. Germans use *Speisekartoffel.*

Overnight Cabbage Slaw
Krautsalat

1 head shredded cabbage
1 minced small onion
1 diced red or green pepper
2 tablespoons celery seed
1/2 teaspoon salt

Dressing:
1 cup sugar
1/2 cup vinegar
1/2 cup vegetable oil

In mixing bowl, combine vegetables, celery seed, and salt. In saucepan, combine sugar, vinegar, and vegetable oil and bring to low boil. Pour over vegetables. Cool. Cover and refrigerate overnight.

Note: This slaw keeps well for several days when refrigerated and can be made ahead.

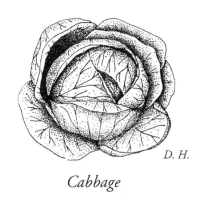

D. H.

Cabbage

Sauerkraut Salad
Sauerkrautsalat

Mary Sharp, Cedar Rapids, Iowa

1 small can sauerkraut (drained)	**Dressing:**
1 cup sliced celery	1/3 cup water
1 cup shredded carrots	2/3 cup vinegar
1 cup diced onion	1/3 cup oil
1 large, diced green pepper	1 cup sugar
	1/4 teaspoon pepper
	Pinch of salt

Mix sauerkraut, celery, carrots, onion, and green pepper ingredients together in salad bowl.

Mix dressing ingredients together in small saucepan and bring to a boil. Pour over the salad ingredients. Let stand at least 8 hours before serving. The salad will keep for three weeks in refrigerator.

Vegetables

Kohl, or cabbage, in its many varieties, is a staple in German cooking. There's *Weiβkohl* (white cabbage), *Rotkohl* (red cabbage), *Grünkohl* (kale), *Blumenkohl* (cauliflower), *Rosenkohl* (Brussels sprouts), *Wirsing* (savoy cabbage), and *Kohlrabi*.

Potatoes, too, are a staple, but it was not automatic. Frederick II the Great (1712–1786) of Prussia was convinced the potato could solve the perennial problems of famine, poverty, and unrest. But the peasants resisted, believing the potato was poisonous. Frederick would have none of that and posted soldiers in the fields, making sure the seed potatoes were planted. Today, potatoes *(Kartoffeln)* are an important side dish and most generally served boiled or mashed with German meals. Leftovers are fried.

Green Beans
Grüne Bohnen

Anneliese Heider Tisdale, Cedar Rapids, Iowa

The summer savory herb gives the beans a good flavor. I grow it in my herb garden and freeze sprigs for use during the winter.

2 pounds green beans	Several sprigs (or 1 teaspoon
1 chopped onion	dried) summer savory herb
Butter	1 beef or chicken bouillon cube
1 tablespoon flour	Salt and pepper to taste
Chopped fresh parsley	

Wash beans, trim ends and cut beans into 1-inch pieces. Simmer beans in salted water for about 10 minutes. Drain beans, saving and cooling the cooking water. In pot, sauté the onion in butter until onion pieces are glassy. Add flour and stir well. Add some of the cooled cooking liquid, the summer savory, the beans, parsley, and bouillon cube. Stir and simmer until beans are tender. Salt and pepper to taste.

Note: I always make extra, because they taste even better the next day.

Green Beans (Frozen)
Eingefrorene Grüne Bohnen

2 packages frozen cut
  green beans
4 slices bacon

1/4 cup diced onion
1 can cream of celery soup
1/3 cup milk

Cook and drain green beans according to package instructions. In a sauce pan, brown bacon until crisp. Drain and crumble. Cook onion in about 2 tablespoons of bacon drippings. Add soup, milk, and beans. Heat and stir often. Before serving, sprinkle with crumbled bacon.

Green Peas and Carrots
Erbsen und Karotten

Anneliese Heider Tisdale, Cedar Rapids, Iowa

My mother used fresh peas and carrots from the garden to prepare this. It was one of my favorite vegetables. Since I don't have a garden anymore, I use frozen peas.

1/2 diced onion
1 tablespoon butter or margarine
2 cups diced carrots
2 cups green peas

Chicken or beef broth
1/4 cup chopped fresh parsley
  or to taste
Salt and pepper to taste

Sauté the onion in butter until glassy but not brown. Add the carrots and continue to sauté over low heat until almost tender. Add the peas and sauté a few minutes more. Add the broth, cover and simmer until vegetables are tender. Add the parsley, salt, and pepper to taste, and serve immediately.

Carrots

D. H.

Carrot Casserole
Karotten Auflauf

2 pounds sliced carrots
1 large chopped onion
Salt and pepper to taste

2 cups shredded Cheddar cheese
2 cups crushed crackers
6 tablespoons butter

Preheat oven to 350°. In saucepan, cover carrots and onion with water and cook until tender crisp, about 8 minutes. Drain. Place carrots and onion into lightly greased 9x13-inch baking dish. Add salt and pepper. Sprinkle with cheese. Cover with crushed crackers. (Ritz® crackers work well.) Melt butter and drizzle over crackers. Bake 30 minutes.

Red Cabbage
Rotkohl

Anneliese Heider Tisdale, Cedar Rapids, Iowa

In Bavaria, where I come from, we call red cabbage *Blaukraut,* or blue cabbage, rather than *Rotkohl.*

3 slices bacon, cut in strips
1 chopped medium onion
1 tart apple
1 finely shredded head red
  cabbage
1 tablespoon sugar

4 tablespoons vinegar
Small glass of red wine (optional)
Beef broth
1 teaspoon salt and pepper
  to taste

In a large saucepan, brown the bacon. Set bacon aside. Drain off most of the bacon grease. In small amount of bacon grease, sauté the onion until it is glassy. Peel, core, and chop apple. Add apple, cabbage, sugar, vinegar, wine, and beef broth. Stir to mix ingredients and simmer, uncovered, for 15 minutes. Cover pan and simmer 20 minutes more or until cabbage is tender. Stir occasionally. Season to taste.

Notes: A small amount of vegetable oil may be used instead of the bacon grease. Red cabbage tastes better if it is made the day before. Reheat on low heat and serve.

Kohlrabi
Kohlrabigemüse

Anneliese Heider Tisdale, Cedar Rapids, Iowa

4 to 6 kohlrabi
1 chopped onion
3 tablespoons butter
2 to 3 tablespoons flour

Chicken or beef broth
1/2 cup fresh chopped parsley
Salt, pepper, and nutmeg to taste

Peel and slice kohlrabi. Cook in salted water until crisp tender. Drain and set kohlrabi aside, but save and cool the cooking liquid. Sauté onion in butter. Add the flour, stirring well to incorporate. Add some of the cooled cooking liquid and broth, making a smooth sauce. Stir well. Add the cooked kohlrabi and parsley. Season with salt, pepper, and nutmeg to taste.

Mashed Potatoes and Crumbs
Kartoffeln und Bröset

6 potatoes
Milk

Butter
1/2 cup bread crumbs

Wash potatoes and cut in chunks. Cover with water and boil till soft, about 30 minutes. Pour off water. Add milk and butter and mash potatoes with electric mixer or by hand. Add bread crumbs. This is good to serve with a meat, like ham, that produces no drippings for gravy.

Pickled Beets
Süßsauere Rote Rüben

3 pounds beets
1 cup sugar
1 cup vinegar

1 cup water
1 teaspoons salt

Wash beets and cover with water. Boil until tender. Pour off water and cover in cold water to cool. Peel and quarter beets. Combine remaining ingredients in saucepan and bring to a boil. Add beets and bring to boil again.

Main Dishes

Germans are meat-eaters, but they tend to eat smaller portions at their main meal and consume much larger quantities of sliced meat, cold-cuts, and wurst (sausages) during their other two meals. Beef traditionally did not play a large role in the German diet until after World War II.

Pork, however, remains king in German cooking. Every bit of the hog is used. It is as popular fresh (as pork roast, cutlets, and hocks) as it is cured. German butchers cure meat traditionally, using natural ingredients. The meat is pickled or salted (sometimes both) and then cold- or warm-smoked. World-renowned examples include German smoked hams and *Kasseler* (smoked pork loin roast).

The favorite German cut of veal is *Schnitzel,* a pork cutlet. It may be breaded *(Wiener Schnitzel),* simmered in sour cream *(Rahmschnitzel),* served with a fried egg and anchovies *(Holsteiner Schnitzel),* or simply pan-fried and served with lemon wedges *(Schnitzel Natur).*

Meat in the form of wurst, sausage and cold-cuts, is offered in far more varieties than Americans see in a typical supermarket.

In general, German wurst is divided into four types. *Rohwurst* is cured and smoked and may be eaten without cooking. *Brühwurst* is smoked and scalded and eaten warm. *Kochwurst* is cooked and sometimes smoked; it corresponds to what Americans call cold-cuts. *Bratwurst,* an American favorite, is a general term for raw wurst that must be cooked before eating.

Also, Germans eat more game than Americans, with rabbit and venison served year-round.

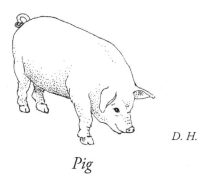

D. H.

Pig

Pork Schnitzel
Schweineschnitzel

Anneliese Heider Tisdale, Cedar Rapids, Iowa

4 pork loin slices, 1/2-inch thick	Bread crumbs
Salt and pepper	Vegetable oil
Flour	Lemon slices
1 egg mixed with 2 tablespoons water	Parsley

Pound cutlets until thin. Sprinkle with salt and pepper. Dredge each cutlet with flour. Lightly beat eggs with water. Dip each cutlet in egg wash and dredge in bread crumbs. Let the breaded cutlets rest for 30 minutes on a sheet of wax paper. Heat oil in skillet and fry cutlets until done, turning once. This takes about 15 minutes. Garnish with lemon slices and parsley sprigs. When served, squeeze the lemon juice over the *Schnitzel*.

Note: Pork Schnitzel is good served with salads and parsley potatoes.

Bratwurst and Rice
Bratwurst und Reis

1 onion	1 chicken bouillon cube
1 teaspoon garlic	1/4 cup warm water
2 tablespoons butter	3 cups uncooked rice
1-1/2 pounds ground bratwurst	6 cups water
1 can sauerkraut	1 teaspoon pepper

In saucepan, sauté onions and garlic in butter. Add bratwurst and cook until brown. Add undrained sauerkraut and heat through. Dissolve bouillon cube in warm water. Add bouillon and rice to brat mixture and stir. Add water and pepper and bring to a boil. Turn down heat and simmer about 30 minutes, until rice is tender.

Grandma's Goetta
Oma's Goetta

Donna Kremer, Camp Springs, Kentucky

1 (3-pound) Boston butt
 pork roast
8 cups water
3 cups pinhead (steel-cut) oats

1 finely chopped large onion
3 teaspoons salt
Pinch of pepper to taste

Cook meat slowly in boiling water about 2 hours. Remove meat and cool, but save water. Grind meat and put back in cooking water. Add rest of ingredients. Cook on low about 2 hours, stirring often to prevent sticking. It will get thick. Cool and pour into greased loaf pans. Refrigerate to set up. Slice and fry in oil, browning on each side until crisp. Serve.

Notes: Other pork cuts can be used, but we like Boston butt best. My sister likes to put maple syrup on her Goetta at the table.

Wiener Schnitzel

The Berghoff Restaurant, Chicago

Wiener Schnitzel is the best-selling entrée at Chicago's famed Berghoff Restaurant. Chilling the breaded culets before frying is the secret to a crisp exterior and juicy interior. Herman Berghoff, the restaurant's third-generation owner, thinks the best way to eat this dish is to squeeze lemon over all of it, then accompany every bite of cutlet with a thin slice of dill pickle.

1 cup flour, seasoned with salt
 and white pepper
2 large, lightly beaten eggs
2 tablespoons milk
1 cup cracker meal or fine
 bread crumbs

4 (5-ounce) veal cutlets,
 pounded thin and chilled
Vegetable oil
Lemon wedges
Kosher dill pickle wedges

Put the seasoned flour in a small bowl. In a shallow container, whisk the eggs and milk together. In a medium-sized bowl, place the cracker meal. Entirely coat each cutlet with the flour, then the egg mixture, and finally the cracker meal. Pat the cutlets with the meal to ensure they are completely coated. Place one layer of cutlets on a baking sheet, cover, and refrigerate at least 30 minutes before cooking.

Pour oil to a depth of 1/4-inch in a large skillet. Heat over medium-high heat. Gently add a few cutlets at a time, and cook until golden brown on both sides, 2 to 3 minutes per side. Transfer to a baking sheet lined with absorbent paper. Keep warm until ready to serve.

Serves four. Serve cutlets on heated plate with a lemon wedge and a pickle wedge. A good side dish is German fries, mashed potatoes, or German potato salad served warm. A simple tossed salad can complete the meal.

BAUERNMARKT
Farmer's Market

MENU

Savory Bread Pudding 3.75
with Spring Peas and Wild Mushroom Ragout

German Meatloaf Sandwich 3.75
with Sweet Mustard and Fried Shallots

Potato Pancake 2.75
with house made Apple Sauce

Hugo – Charles De Fere "Organic" Brut   6.50
with Elderflower and Mint

	6oz	12oz
Florida Avenue American Wheat Ale	3.50	6.75
Krombacher Hefeweizen	3.50	6.75
Goose Island Brewing Company's Honker Ale	3.50	6.75
Blue Point's Toasted Lager	3.50	6.75

Beer Flight 13.00

- Florida Avenue American Wheat Ale
- Krombacher Hefeweizen
- Honker Ale
- Toasted Lager

Dasani Bottled Water 2.50
Seagram's Orange Citrus Sparkling Water .. 2.75
Minute Maid Light Lemonade 2.75
Honest Kids' Super Fruit Punch 2.75

Bauernmarkt Farmer's Market menu sign

The following three recipes are variations of *Rouladen*.

Beef Roll-Ups
Rindsrouladen

Anneliese Heider Tisdale, Cedar Rapids, Iowa

Bacon slices
Dill pickles
3 pounds boneless beef sirloin
 steak, cut about 1/4-inch
 thick, trimmed of fat
Small jar German-style mustard
 (or Grey Poupon)
Vegetable oil
3 cups beef stock

1 bay leaf
1 envelope dry onion soup
4 tablespoons flour
1 cup water
1 cup sour cream
Salt and pepper to taste
1 teaspoon instant coffee
 (optional)

Cut the bacon slices in half and precook in microwave to eliminate some of the fat. Cut dill pickles in half lengthwise, and quarter them if pickles are large. Put a thin layer of mustard on each slice of meat. Put a slice of bacon down the center. Lay a pickle on top and roll up. Fasten each roll-up with a strong toothpick or a metal poultry skewer. Heat a small amount of vegetable oil in large skillet and brown the roll-ups. Place browned roll-ups in large pot or slow cooker.

Heat the beef broth. Mix broth, bay leaf and onion soup mix together and pour over roll-ups. Simmer until meat is tender. (The roll-ups also can be baked in covered casserole in oven.) When meat is tender, discard bay leaf and remove roll-ups to a warm serving dish.

Make a paste of flour and about a cup of water and add to the cooking liquid. Cook until gravy is thick. Add sour cream and heat through but do not boil. (It's optional, but I add instant coffee for a rich flavor.) Return roll-ups to gravy and heat through.

Notes: Roll-ups are usually served with *Spätzle* (see recipe in this book), bread dumplings, or wide noodles. Red cabbage is often served with roll-ups. Also, I call the meat man a day ahead so he can cut the meat for this recipe while the meat is frozen.

Rouladen

Erika Bandows, Big Bear Lake, California

2 pounds of round steak, about
  8 pieces
1/4 cup German or Dijon mustard
8 strips of bacon

8 dill pickle wedges
1 large onion, cut into wedges
3 tablespoons vegetable oil
3 cups beef broth

Cut or pound round steak to 1/4-inch thickness. Spread mustard on each slice. Sprinkle with salt and pepper. Place slice of bacon, a pickle wedge and an onion wedge on each slice. Roll up. Close and secure with toothpicks. Heat oil in frying pan and brown meat on each side. Add beef broth, bring to boil and then reduce heat. Cover and simmer for 1-1/2 hours or until tender.

Note: We usually serve with gravy, red cabbage, and boiled potatoes.

Anna Theresia's Incredible *Rouladen*

Monika Taylor, Germantown, Maryland

I obtained this recipe from my mother the weekend before she died in April 2011. Of all the wonderful German/Austrian meals she prepared, this is by far the one we loved the most.

8 to 10 thin slices of beef, about
  1 foot in length
2 to 3 pickles
1/2 white onion

3 to 4 slices bacon
Shortening (like Crisco®)
Mustard

Lay meat flat on cutting board. Slice pickles, onion, and cooked bacon into small pieces. Evenly distribute mixture on beef slices. Roll the meat around the ingredients and add a toothpick at the end of the roll to hold it together.

Heat shortening and slowly brown the meat, being careful not to burn it. When the juices begin to gather in the pan, add a small amount of water (not more than 1/4 cup) to make gravy. Add flour to the juices to make "gravy eyes." Cook the meat on medium heat until well done. Add mustard lightly over the cooked meat before serving.

Breaded Pork Loins
Karbonade

2 eggs
2 tablespoons milk
8 pork tenderloins

1/2 cup bread crumbs
1/3 cup shortening
Salt and pepper to taste

Preheat oven to 325°. In a bowl, beat eggs and milk. Dredge loins in egg mixture and then bread crumbs. Melt shortening in skillet and brown loins on both sides. Put meat in pan or casserole, cover and bake for 1 hour. Serves 4 to 6.

Chicken Schnitzel
Hühnerschnitzel

Shirley Ruedy, Cedar Rapids, Iowa

4 (6-ounce) chicken cutlets
Salt and pepper
1/2 to 1 cup flour
2 eggs beaten with 2 tablespoons
    water

1 to 2 cups dried white bread
    crumbs
Peanut oil (best of the vegetable
    oils for non-spatter)
1 lemon cut in wedges

You can find 6-ounce chicken cutlets at most staffed supermarket meat counters (not the prepackaged cases). Or you can make them by cutting and pressing large, skinless chicken breasts to desired thickness. Cutlets should be 5- to 6-inch oblong pieces. To prepare cutlets, preheat about 4 inches of oil in a deep sauté pan or deep-fat fryer. Season cutlets with salt and pepper on each side and dredge in flour. In bowl, beat eggs and water. Dip breaded cutlets in egg mixture. Coat with bread crumbs on both sides. Deep fry cutlets about three minutes or until golden brown on each side and cooked through. Drain on paper towels. Blot excess oil. Serve with lemon wedges.

Reuben Meatloaf
Reuben Hackbraten

1 pound ground beef
12 ounces corned beef
2-1/2 cups soft bread crumbs
2 eggs
2 tablespoons minced onion
8 ounces sauerkraut

1/2 teaspoon caraway seeds
(optional)
1 cup shredded Swiss cheese
2 slices Swiss cheese
Thousand Island salad dressing
(optional)

Preheat oven to 350°. Finely chop corned beef and set aside. Drain and finely chop sauerkraut and set aside. In mixing bowl, mix together ground beef, corned beef, bread crumbs, eggs, and onion. Pat mixture into a 15x12-inch rectangle on a sheet of plastic wrap. Put sauerkraut on top of meat, within 1 inch of edge. Sprinkle on caraway seeds and shredded cheese. Roll tightly, sealing ends and edges. Place seam side down in baking dish. Bake 45 to 60 minutes. When done, place Swiss cheese slices on top of loaf to melt. Let stand 5 to 10 minutes. Can be served with Thousand Island dressing.

German Cabbage Burgers
Kohl Burger

1 package frozen dinner rolls
1 pound ground beef
1/2 cup chopped onion
1/2 teaspoon garlic salt

1/2 teaspoon salt
3 cups shredded cabbage
1/3 cup cold water
1 tablespoon flour

Thaw dinner rolls overnight. Preheat oven to 375°. In skillet, brown meat, onion, garlic salt, and salt. Drain off grease. Put shredded cabbage over meat. Cover and cook until cabbage is tender, about 10 minutes. In small bowl or measuring cup, combine water and flour.

Pour into meat mixture and stir until thickened over low heat. Remove skillet from heat. With rolling pin, roll out each dinner roll until it's about a 4-inch circle. Put about 1/4 cup of meat-cabbage filling in the middle of each roll. Dampen edges of dough with water and fold in half. Seal edges with a fork. Put each "burger" in greased baking dish or rimmed cookie sheet. Bake 15 to 20 minutes until brown.

Hamburger-Sauerkraut Casserole
Hackfleisch-Sauerkraut Auflauf

1 small diced onion
1 tablespoon butter
1 pound hamburger
1 can mushroom soup

1 can cream of celery soup
1 small can sauerkraut
3/4 cup dry noodles
1 cup grated mild Cheddar cheese

Preheat oven to 350°. In skillet, sauté onion in butter until glassy. Add hamburger and brown. Pour off excess grease. Put half of burger mixture into casserole dish. To other half of burger mixture, add soups, sauerkraut, and noodles. Mix together and add to casserole dish. Bake 30 minutes. Take out of oven and cover with grated cheese. (Any variety of cheese can be substituted.) Return casserole dish to oven and bake another 10 minutes.

Beef and Cabbage Casserole
Hackfleisch und Kohl Auflauf

Medium head of cabbage
1-1/2 pounds ground beef
1 diced medium onion
Salt and pepper to taste

3 tablespoons uncooked rice
1 can tomato soup
1 can water

Preheat oven to 350°. Chop up cabbage and place in large, lightly greased casserole dish. In a saucepan, brown beef and onion. Pour off excess grease. Season with salt and pepper. Add rice, soup, and water to meat mixture and bring to a boil. Pour mixture over cabbage but don't stir. Cover casserole and bake 60 to 90 minutes, until cabbage is tender.

D. H.

Sliced Cabbage

Fried Beef Dumplings
Fleischküchle

8 ounces lean hamburger
1 small diced onion
Salt and pepper to taste
6 cups flour

2 teaspoons salt
3 eggs
2 cups milk
Oil for deep frying

In medium bowl, blend together hamburger, onion, salt, and pepper. In a large bowl, combine flour and salt. Add eggs and milk, blending well. Form the dough into 2-inch balls. On a clean, floured surface, roll out each ball of dough into a circle about 1/4-inch thick.

Shape the burger mixture into balls a little more than 1-inch in diameter. Place each ball into a circle of dough. Fold the dough to encircle the meat. Seal the edges with your fingers. Preheat oil in skillet over medium-high heat (or to 370 degrees in deep-fat fryer). Fry the *Kuechle* until golden brown, turning once. Serve warm.

Ham Balls
Schinkenkugeln

2 eggs
1/3 cup catsup
1 pound ground ham
1 pound ground beef
1 cup milk
1 cup cubed bread

Sauce:
1 cup firmly packed brown sugar
1/2 cup vinegar
1/2 cup water
1 teaspoon mustard

Lightly grease flat cake pan or rectangular casserole dish. In large mixing bowl, blend together eggs and catsup. Add ham, ground beef, milk, and bread cubes. Mix well. Shape mixture into balls about 1-inch in diameter. Place in baking dish. Turn on oven and preheat to 350°. In saucepan, blend together brown sugar, vinegar, water, and mustard. Bring to boil and simmer for 20 minutes. Pour sauce over ham balls. Bake 60 minutes.

Ham Loaf
Schinken Laib

1 egg
3/4 cup milk
2 pounds ground ham
1 cup graham cracker crumbs
Salt and pepper to taste

Sauce:
3/4 cup firmly packed
   brown sugar
1/2 cup tomato juice
1 teaspoon dry mustard
2 tablespoons vinegar

Preheat oven to 325°. Lightly grease or spray loaf pan. In mixing bowl, blend egg and milk. Add ham, graham cracker crumbs, and seasoning. Mix well. Shape into loaf and place in loaf pan. In separate bowl, mix together brown sugar, tomato juice, dry mustard, and vinegar. Pour over loaf. Bake 90 minutes.

Ham Baked in Bread
Schinken im Brotteig gebacken

Jack and Doris Hahn, Middle Amana, Iowa

1 recipe for basic bread dough
1 (14-pound) precooked ham

Melted butter
1 egg

Roll out half the dough to about 15 inches in diameter, or large enough to cover the bottom and two-thirds up the sides of the ham. Place dough on a large greased baking sheet. With a brush (or your fingers), moisten 2 to 3 inches of the outer edge of the circle of dough.

Place the ham in the center of the dough. Roll out the second half of the dough to the same size, and place over the ham. Pull the bottom dough up over the edge of the top dough. Press hard all around to make the dough stick together. Brush the entire ball with melted butter to keep the dough soft.

Let rise in warm place for about 45 to 60 minutes or until dough doubles in bulk. Seal any cracks in the dough by pressing the cracks together with a little water.

Preheat oven to 375 degrees. Beat egg. Brush the entire ball with the beaten egg. Bake in preheated oven for 1 hour and 45 minutes. Cover lightly with foil if it begins to brown too much before the baking time is up.

Roast Goose
Gänsebraten

Hank Shaw, Sacramento, California

Germans traditionally served roast goose at Christmas, though turkey has replaced goose on many tables. If you'd like to try a goose for a holiday dinner, you'll find excellent directions and how-to pictures on *Hank Shaw's Hunter Angler Gardener Cook* blog. This somewhat shortened version is reprinted with his permission and that of Elisa Bauer, founder of the *Simply Cooking* blog, where the recipe also appears.

3–4 cups root vegetables such as (carrots, parsnips, turnips, potatoes, and/or rutabagas)	1 head garlic
	Gravy:
	Goose giblets and wings
1 goose, approximately 8 pounds	1/2 cup Madeira wine
Juice of 1 lemon	2 tablespoons flour
Salt and pepper	2 cups chicken stock (for gravy)
1/2 peeled and chopped yellow onion	1 teaspoon dried thyme

Peel and chop the root vegetables (such as carrots, parsnips, turnips, potatoes, and/or rutabagas).

If goose is frozen, defrost in refrigerator for two days. When thawed, put goose in a pan (to catch any leaks) and bring goose to room temperature, keeping it in its plastic wrapping until you are ready to cook.

Prepare goose: Remove the neck and giblets and the last two joints of the wings; save these for making gravy. Slice off the neck skin about a half-inch in front of the body. Slice off goose's tail.

Remove excess fat from goose cavity (you can save for a healthy cooking fat). Slice off wide belly flaps covering the body cavity and discard. Prick the goose's outside skin with a clean needle—you have to give the fat underneath the skin someplace to go so the skin can crisp up. Do this all over the goose.

—199

Preheat the oven to 325°. Rub the goose all over with the cut half of a lemon. Use both halves to coat well. Put the lemon halves inside the goose. Sprinkle outside of goose with salt, using more than you think you need since it helps crisp the skin and adds flavor.

Slice off the top of a head of garlic and put inside the goose. Place the goose breast-side up on a rack in a roasting pan and place in the oven. Use a pan that's big enough to accommodate root vegetables, which you'll add after about 20 minutes.

Start the gravy: Chop and brown all giblets, wings, and neck in goose fat in a large pan. Sprinkle with salt. Add the chopped onion and stir. When the onion is a little brown, sprinkle flour in the pan and stir to combine. Cook over medium heat, stirring often, until it smells nutty—about 5 to 10 minutes. Turn up the heat to high and add the Madeira. Boil furiously for a minute or two. Add chicken stock and stir to combine. Add dried thyme. Turn down heat to a bare simmer. Watch it; if it gets too thick, add a little water.

Add vegetables: After goose has cooked 20 minutes, add chunked root vegetables to roasting pan. Tip: Toss the vegetables in rendered goose fat and salt them before placing in the bottom of the roasting pan. Spoon out some of the goose fat that may be collecting in bottom of roasting pan. (You can save and reuse the fat.) Return goose to oven for another 25 minutes. Test temperature of breast. You want it between 130 and 140 degrees. Remove from oven (but keep oven on).

Carve off breasts: With a thin boning knife, slice along the keel bone, which separates the two halves of the breast. Free the side of the breast with short, gentle strokes (see Hank's blog for pictures on how to do this). Remove the breasts and tent with aluminum foil.

Finish roasting: Return the rest of the goose and vegetables to the oven. Cook another 45 minutes until the thigh reaches 165–175 degrees on a meat thermometer. Remove from oven. Test root vegetables for doneness and return to oven if still hard. Remove garlic clove from goose cavity. Tent the goose with foil and set aside.

Finish gravy: Remove garlic cloves from husk and put the cloves into the simmering gravy. Cook for 5 minutes. Fish out the neck and wing pieces and pick off bits of meat and return to gravy. Pour gravy in blender and blend on high. You want a thick gravy, but if it is too thick, add water. Return gravy to pot and put on low heat. Simmer if gravy is too thin.

Sear breasts: Heat a large sauté pan to hot. Add goose fat and heat over medium-high heat. Pat dry goose breasts. Place skin side down in pan and sear 3 to 4 minutes to achieve a rich brown skin. Press down to get good contact. Remove breasts. (Don't sear meat side.) Immediately salt the skin. Set aside, skin side up.

Carve: Carve off legs and wings. Get the sauté pan hot again and sear skin surfaces (only) of legs and wings. While searing, slice breast at an angle. Salt the legs and wings when done.

Serve: Put the gravy under the meat. Serve with vegetables. You can save the bones to make goose stock which is used just like chicken stock.

D. H.

Goose

Desserts and Drinks

Several world-famous cake recipes originated in Germany. The best known is likely the Black Forest Cherry Cake, a magnificent layered composition of spongy chocolate cake, cherries, and whipped cream.

Germany also is known for its tortes—layer cakes with fillings of whipped cream and other delights. The cakes are very rich, but generally they are not as sweet as American cakes. Germans often glaze their cakes rather than cover them in thick icing or frosting.

"Health" Cake
Gesundheitskuchen

Anneliese Heider Tisdale, Cedar Rapids, Iowa

We had this on Sunday mornings during my childhood in Germany.

1 stick butter or margarine	2 teaspoons baking powder
1/2 cup vegetable shortening	1 cup milk
1-3/4 cups sugar	1 grated and juiced lemon
4 eggs	1/2 cup raisins, soaked in rum for
2-1/2 cups sifted flour	several hours or overnight

Preheat oven to 350°. Grease and flour a *Gugelhupf* or Bundt cake pan. Cream together butter, shortening, and sugar. Add eggs, one at a time, and cream well. Add grated lemon zest and juice. Sift together flour and baking powder. Gradually add flour mixture, alternating with milk. Coat raisins with a little flour. Fold in just enough to have a smooth batter. Pour in cake pan, and bake for 60 to 65 minutes.

Black Forest Cherry Cake
Schwarzwälder Kirschtorte

Irma Parrott, Iowa City, Iowa

1 (4-ounce) package Baker's German's Sweet Chocolate®
1/2 cup boiling water
1 cup butter or margarine
2 cups sugar
4 egg yolks
1 teaspoon vanilla
2-1/4 cups flour
1 teaspoon baking soda
1/2 teaspoon salt
1 cup buttermilk
4 stiffly beaten egg whites

Filling:
2 (16-ounce) cans pitted tart red cherries, drained
1/2 cup kirsch (cherry brandy), divided
2 cups whipping cream
1/2 cup powdered sugar

Assembly:
3 ounces finely grated semisweet chocolate
16 maraschino cherries, drained

Preheat oven to 350°. In a small saucepan, melt the chocolate in the boiling water. Cool. Cream the butter and the sugar until fluffy. Add the egg yolks, one at a time, beating well after each. Blend in the vanilla and the melted chocolate. Sift the flour with the baking soda and salt; add alternately with the buttermilk to the chocolate mixture, beating after each addition until smooth. Fold in the beaten egg whites. Pour the batter into three 9-inch layer pans lined with waxed paper on the bottom. Bake for 30 to 35 minutes. Cool.

Filling: Drain the cherries and cut each in half. Combine the cherries and 1/3 cup kirsch. Let the cherries soak while baking the cake, then drain, reserving the kirsch. With a fork, prick the top of each cooled cake layer and spoon the reserved kirsch over the cake layers. Whip the cream until almost stiff, then add the powdered sugar and the remaining kirsch, and continue whipping until stiff. Place one cake layer on a cake plate. Spread with one-fourth of the whipped cream and top with half of the drained cherries. Repeat. Then top with the third layer.

Assembly: Frost the side of the cake with half of the remaining whipped cream. Using your hand, gently press the grated chocolate into the cream. Garnish the top of the cake with the remaining whipped cream and place the maraschino cherries in a circle around the top of the cake. Keep the cake refrigerated but do not cover. Serves 12 to 16.

Gingerbread
Lebkuchen

Mary Sharp, Cedar Rapids, Iowa

2-1/3 cups flour	3/4 teaspoon salt
1/3 cup sugar	1/2 cup vegetable shortening
1 teaspoon baking soda	1 egg
1 teaspoon ginger	1 cup molasses
1 teaspoon cinnamon	3/4 cup hot water

Preheat oven to 325°. Grease and flour 9x9-inch pan. Put all ingredients into large mixing bowl. Using electric mixer, beat ingredients on low speed for 30 seconds, then on medium speed for 3 minutes. Scrape mixture off sides of bowl as you go. Pour batter into pan. Bake about 50 minutes, until wooden toothpick inserted in center comes out clean.

Note: This is delicious served with whipped cream or ice cream. For a variation, beat together (till stiff) 2 cups whipping cream, 1/4 cup honey, and 1/2 teaspoon ginger.

Cinnamon Cake
Zimt-Kuchen

1/2 cup butter	3 cups flour
1/2 cup shortening	3 teaspoons baking powder
2 cups sugar	1 teaspoon salt
4 eggs	2 tablespoons cinnamon
1 cup milk	1/3 cup sugar
2 teaspoons vanilla	

Preheat oven to 350°. Grease a 10-inch tube pan and set aside. Cream together butter and shortening in a large bowl. Gradually add and beat in 2 cups sugar until fluffy. Add eggs, one at a time, beating well after each one. In a small bowl, mix together milk and vanilla. On wax paper, sift together flour, baking powder and salt. Alternately add flour mixture and milk mixture to butter/egg mixture, beating well after each addition.

Combine cinnamon and 1/3 cup of sugar; sprinkle about two teaspoons of cinnamon mixture into the greased tube pan. Add one-third of batter. Spread another two teaspoons of cinnamon mixture on top of batter. Repeat twice. Bake for 75 minutes or until brown and toothpick comes out clean. Cool 10 minutes. Remove from pan to baking rack.

Cake can be topped with powdered sugar glaze. For glaze: Beat together 1-1/4 cups powdered sugar and approximately 3 tablespoons of milk, beating well after adding each tablespoon until achieving semi-translucent glaze consistency.

Applesauce Cake
Apfelmuskuchen

Diana Pesek, Cedar Rapids, Iowa

1/2 cup melted butter	1-1/2 teaspoons salt
2 cups sugar	2-1/2 teaspoons cinnamon
1 large egg	2 teaspoons ground cloves
1-1/2 cups applesauce	2 teaspoons allspice
2-3/4 cups flour	1/2 cup water
1-1/2 teaspoons (barely) baking soda	1 cup chopped walnuts
	1 cup raisins

Preheat oven to 350°. Grease a tube cake pan with butter and line bottom with waxed paper. Set aside. In large mixing bowl, beat together melted butter and sugar. Add egg and applesauce and mix well. Add in rest of ingredients, mixing well as you go. Fold in walnuts and raisins at the last. Pour into prepared cake pan. Bake for 60 to 70 minutes. Check for doneness with toothpick.

German Sweet Chocolate Cake

This classic recipe comes from Baker's German's Sweet Chocolate®

1 bar (4 ounces) Baker's German's
   Sweet Chocolate®
1/2 cup boiling water
1 cup butter or margarine
2 cups sugar
4 egg yolks

1 teaspoon vanilla
2-1/2 cups flour
1/2 teaspoon salt
1 teaspoon baking soda
1 cup buttermilk
4 stiffly beaten egg whites

Preheat oven to 350°. Line bottoms of three deep 8- or 9-inch layer cake pans with waxed paper or parchment paper. To begin, melt chocolate bar in boiling water. Cool. In large mixing bowl, cream together butter and sugar until fluffy. Add egg yolks, one at a time, beating well after each. Add melted chocolate and vanilla. Mix well. Sift together flour, salt, and baking soda. Add alternately with buttermilk to chocolate mixture. Beat well and until smooth. Fold in egg whites. Pour into three cake pans. Bake 30 to 40 minutes. Cool. Frost tops only with Coconut-Pecan Frosting (below).

Coconut-Pecan Frosting

1 cup evaporated milk
1 cup sugar
3 egg yolks
1/2 cup butter or margarine

1 teaspoon vanilla
1-1/3 cups coconut
1 cup chopped pecans

Combine ingredients in medium saucepan. Cook and stir over medium heat until thickened, about 12 minutes. Remove from heat. Then add the coconut and pecans.

    Beat together until thick enough to spread. Makes 2-1/2 cups. Frost tops only of German's Sweet Chocolate Cake and stack the layers.

Rhubarb Cake
Rhabarberkuchen

1/2 cup butter or margarine
1 egg
1 cup firmly packed brown sugar
1 cup sugar
1 cup milk
2 cups flour

1 teaspoon baking soda
2 cups diced raw rhubarb

Topping:
3/4 cup sugar
1 teaspoon cinnamon

Preheat oven to 350°. In mixing bowl, cream together butter, egg, and sugars. Add milk and mix. Sift together flour and baking soda and add to butter mixture. Mix well. Fold in rhubarb pieces. Pour into 9x13-inch cake pan. Mix sugar and cinnamon together for topping and put on cake before baking. Bake 30 to 35 minutes.

Snicker Cake
Snickerkuchen

1 German chocolate cake mix
1 package (14 ounces) caramels
1/3 cup milk

1 stick butter or margarine
3/4 cup chocolate chips
1 cup pecans

Preheat oven to 350°. Grease 9x13-inch pan. Prepare cake according to directions. Pour half the batter into pan. Bake 20 minutes and remove cake from oven. (Lower oven temperature to 250°.) Melt caramels, milk, and butter in microwave. Pour caramel mixture on top of cake. Sprinkle with chocolate chips and pecans. Spread remaining batter over top. Bake 20 minutes at 250°. Turn up oven to 350° and bake another 10 to 15 minutes. Serve with whipped cream or ice cream. Cake can be iced, if you want.

Apple Strudel
Apfelstreusel

The Berghoff Restaurant, Chicago

1-1/4 cups apple juice

2 tablespoons cornstarch

1/2 pound Granny Smith apples, peeled, cored, and sliced 1/4-inch thick (5 cups)

1/2 cup dark seedless raisins

3 tablespoons granulated sugar

1 teaspoon ground cinnamon

1/3 cup chopped pecans

4 sheets phyllo dough

1/3 cup (5-1/3 tablespoons) melted butter

3 tablespoons fine dry bread crumbs

Confectioners' sugar, for garnish

Vanilla ice cream

In a small bowl, create a slurry by combining 1/4 cup of the apple juice with 2 tablespoons of cornstarch; mix until smooth and set aside. In a large saucepan over medium heat, cook the apples with the remaining apple juice, and the raisins, sugar, and cinnamon until the apples are tender, 8 to 10 minutes. Stir the cornstarch slurry (it may have settled) and add to the apple mixture, stirring constantly until smooth and lump free. Simmer 1 more minute, stirring constantly. Remove from the heat and cool. Stir in the pecans, cover, and chill.

Preheat oven to 450°. Line a baking sheet with parchment paper. Lay out one phyllo sheet on a clean, flat, lightly floured surface. Brush with melted butter and sprinkle with 1 tablespoon of dry bread crumbs. Repeat this procedure with two more layers of phyllo, butter, and crumbs.

Top with the fourth sheet of phyllo. Spread the apple filling evenly onto phyllo surface, leaving a 1/2-inch clean edge on all sides. Roll into a log, folding edges at each end beneath the log, and brush with melted butter. Carefully place the strudel on the prepared baking sheet, seam side down. Bake the strudel for 15 to 18 minutes, or until golden brown.

Remove from the oven and cool for 15 minutes before cutting into 2-inch slices and sprinkling with confectioners' sugar just before serving. Serve plain or with ice cream. Serves 6 to 8.

Note: The Berghoff chefs will substitute dried bread cake crumbs for bread crumbs, using what is saved after its cooks level the tops of cakes before frosting. Strudel is best served the same day it is baked, and warming it for 10 minutes in a 350°F oven (never in a microwave) enhances it, especially when it's served with a scoop of vanilla ice cream. The dessert takes its name from the flaky pastry that wraps around the filling like a Strudel, the old German word for whirlpool or vortex. In Germany, it was a traditional harvest-time dessert. The thin pastry originated with the Turks. **See the back cover photograph of the Berghoff Apple Strudel.**

Apple Crisp
Apfel Knackig

8 cups sliced apples

1 cup sugar

1 teaspoon cinnamon

1 tablespoon flour

1 cup oatmeal

1 cup flour

1 cup firmly packed brown sugar

1 teaspoon baking powder

1/2 cup melted butter

Preheat oven to 350°. Wash, peel, core, and slice apples. Spray 9x13-inch cake pan and line with uncooked apple slices. Combine sugar, cinnamon, and 1 tablespoon flour and sprinkle over apples. In mixing bowl, combine oatmeal, 1 cup flour, brown sugar, baking powder, and butter. Mix well and crumble mixture over apples. Bake 40 minutes. Many cooks like to serve this warm with vanilla ice cream on top.

Easter Bunny Cookies
Osterhasen Plätzchen

4 large eggs

1-1/8 cups firmly packed brown
   sugar

1-1/8 cups sugar

4 cups flour

1/4 teaspoon baking powder

1/4 teaspoon baking soda

2 to 3 tablespoons melted butter

Preheat oven to 350°. Beat eggs. Add brown sugar and sugar and beat with electric mixer at high speed for 5 minutes. Sift together flour, baking powder and baking soda. Add to eggs slowly and keep beating. Add melted butter and mix. Roll dough out of floured counter or pastry cloth to about 3/8-inch thick. Cut dough into bunny shapes or use bunny cookie cutter. Place on greased cookie sheet or on cookie sheet covered with parchment paper. Bake for 15 to 20 minutes.

Macaroons
Makronen

6 egg whites
2 cups sugar

4 cups coconut
4 tablespoons flour

Preheat oven to 325°. Beat egg whites. Add sugar gradually, then coconut and flour. Drop dough by teaspoons onto greased cookie sheet or onto cookie sheet covered with parchment paper. Bake 12 to 15 minutes.

Soft Butter Cookies
Weiche Butter Kekse

8 eggs
3 cups sugar
2 sticks (1/2 pound) butter or
   margarine

6-1/2 cups flour
1 teaspoon salt
1 teaspoon baking soda
2 teaspoons baking powder

Preheat oven to 350°. Melt butter. Cream together eggs, sugar, and butter. Sift together dry ingredients and gradually add to egg mixture, beating well. Drop by teaspoons on to ungreased cookie sheet or cookie sheet covered with parchment paper. Bake 8 to 10 minutes. Cookies will be firm but not brown. Do not overbake. Makes about 60 cookies.

Note: Batter can be divided and made into different types of cookies. You can add 1 teaspoon melted chocolate and 1 teaspoon vanilla, for example, to make a chocolate cookie. Or you could add coconut.

D. H.

Flowers

Oatmeal Cookies
Haferflocken Kekse

Mary Sharp, Cedar Rapids, Iowa

3/4 cup softened vegetable
  shortening
1 cup firmly packed brown sugar
1/2 cup sugar
1 egg
1/4 cup water

1 teaspoon vanilla
1 cup flour
1 teaspoon salt
1/2 teaspoon baking soda
3 cups uncooked oats

Preheat oven to 350°. In bowl, mix together shortening, sugars, egg, water, and vanilla. Sift together flour, salt, and baking soda. Add to shortening mixture and mix well. Blend in oats. Drop dough by teaspoons on to cookie sheet. Bake for 12 to 15 minutes.

Note: Nuts, raisins, chocolate chips, or coconut can be added for variety.

Refrigerator Cookies
Kühlbox Kekse

Mary Sharp, Cedar Rapids, Iowa

3/4 cup softened butter
1 cup sugar
1 cup firmly packed brown sugar
1 egg
1 teaspoon vanilla

1 cup flour
1/2 teaspoon baking soda
1/2 teaspoon cream of tartar
1/2 cup chopped walnuts
  (optional)

In mixing bowl, cream together butter and sugars. Add egg and vanilla and mix well. Sift together flour, baking soda, and cream of tartar. Add to sugar mixture and mix well. If dough seems too soft, add a little flour. Divide dough and mold into rolls about 1-1/2 inches in diameter. Wrap rolls in waxed paper and refrigerate overnight or until ready to use. Dough can be frozen. When ready to bake cookies, preheat oven to 400°. Slice dough into 1- to 4-inch-wide pieces. Place on cookie sheet. Bake 8 to 10 minutes or until light brown.

Date Cookies
Dattel Kekse

2 eggs
1 cup sugar
1 cup flour
1/2 teaspoon baking powder

1/4 teaspoon cinnamon
1 cup chopped dates
1 cup chopped nuts
Powdered sugar

Preheat oven to 325 degrees. Beat eggs and sugar together. Sift together flour, baking powder, and cinnamon. Add to egg mixture and mix well. Fold in chopped dates and nuts. Spread onto greased baking pan. Bake for 15 to 20 minutes until firm. Cut into 1-by-2-inch bars and roll in powdered sugar.

Fencelatch Cookies
Fenceriegel Kekse

2-1/2 cups flour
1 teaspoon baking soda
1 teaspoon salt
1/2 cup firmly packed brown
   sugar

1/2 cup vegetable shortening
3/4 cup buttermilk
1 egg white (optional)

Preheat oven to 350°. Sift together flour, baking soda, and salt. Add brown sugar. Cut in shortening. Add buttermilk to form a soft dough. Roll out dough to 1/2-inch thickness on floured countertop or pastry cloth. Cut dough into 2-inch squares or diamonds or any design desired. Put on greased cookie sheet. Bake 10 minutes. Tops of cookies can be brushed with egg whites before baking. Makes around 3 to 4 dozen cookies.

D. H.

Flowers

Chocolate Cookies
Schokoladen Kekse

1/2 cup softened butter	1 (4-ounce) sweet chocolate bar
2 cups firmly packed brown sugar	4 cups flour
5 eggs	1 teaspoon soda

Preheat oven to 325°. Melt chocolate bar and cool. Cream together butter and sugar. Beat in eggs, one at a time. Add melted chocolate. Sift together flour and baking soda and add to chocolate mixture. Mix well. Drop by teaspoons onto greased cookie sheet. Bake 12 to 15 minutes.

Snickerdoodles
Zimtplätzchen

2-3/4 cups flour	Topping:
3 teaspoons baking powder	4 teaspoons cinnamon
1/2 teaspoon salt	4 tablespoons sugar
1-1/2 cups sugar	
1 cup softened butter	
2 eggs	

Sift together flour, baking powder, and salt. In mixing bowl, cream together butter and 1-1/2 cups sugar. Beat eggs and add to sugar-butter mixture. Gradually add dry ingredients and mix well. Chill in refrigerator. When ready to make cookies, preheat oven to 400°. Mold dough into small balls, using about a tablespoon for each ball. Roll balls in sugar and cinnamon mixture and place on cookie sheet about 2 inches apart. Bake for 10 minutes.

D. H.

Flowers

Strawberry Shortcake
Erdbeerkuchen

Mary Sharp, Cedar Rapids, Iowa

1 egg	3 tablespoons milk (or cream)
3 tablespoons sugar	2 teaspoons baking powder
1 tablespoon softened butter	1 cup flour (approximate)

Preheat oven to 450°. In mixing bowl, beat egg. Add sugar, butter, milk, and baking powder, mixing well. Add flour to stiffen. Press into 8x8-inch pan. Bake 10 to 15 minutes or until golden brown. Cut into squares. Split squares and top each half with fresh, split strawberries and whipped cream.

Note: If desired: About an hour before serving, put sugar over the strawberries and refrigerate them to make them sweeter and juicier.

Aunt Louise's Christmas Fudge

Shirley Ruedy, Cedar Rapids, Iowa

2 cups sugar	2 (6-ounce) packages
3/4 cup evaporated milk	chocolate chips
2 tablespoons butter or margarine	1 teaspoon vanilla
1/2 teaspoon salt	3/4 cup to 2 cups chopped nuts

Bring sugar, milk, butter, and salt to a boil, stirring continuously. Boil for 2 minutes. Remove from heat and add chocolate chips, vanilla, and nuts. Stir until chips are melted. Pour into buttered, 8-inch square pan. Chill until firm. Cut into small pieces.

Note: This is quite rich and the best fudge recipe I've ever found. You can use any kind of nuts, but black walnuts are best.

Peach Streusel Pie
Pfirsich Streusel

4 cups ripe peaches
1/2 cup firmly packed
   brown sugar
1/2 cup flour
1/2 cup butter
1/2 cup sugar

1/4 teaspoon nutmeg
1 egg
2 tablespoons half and half
   (or milk)
1 teaspoon vanilla

Wash, peel, core, and slice peaches. Preheat oven to 400°. Combine brown sugar and flour. Cut in butter until mixture is coarse and crumbly. Sprinkle half of crumb mixture onto bottom and sides of pie plate, pressing until firm. Add sliced peaches to pie shell. Sprinkle with sugar and nutmeg. In small mixing bowl, mix together egg, half and half, and vanilla. Pour over peaches. Top with remaining crumb mixture. Bake 40 to 45 minutes.

Pharisees' Coffee
Pharisäer

Karin Gottier, Tolland, Connecticut

The story about this drink goes that a pastor was attending a banquet after officiating at a wedding. Everyone knew he did not approve of alcohol, so the hosts came up with this recipe to disguise their spiked coffee. The pastor, after enjoying a cup, raised his finger and said, "Oh, you Pharisees!" The name stuck.

Very strong coffee
Rum

Sugar cubes
Sweetened whipped cream

Rinse tall cups with hot water. Fill about half-way full with very strong, hot coffee. Add 1-1/2-ounces of rum (or to taste) and two lumps of sugar to each cup. Stir. Top with whipped cream. (It's best not to use prepared whipped toppings or artificial whipped cream.)

Cold Duck
Kalte Ente

Anneliese Heider Tisdale, Cedar Rapids, Iowa

1 lemon rind and juice
3 tablespoons sugar
1 cup cognac or brandy
1 bottle (750 ml) chilled
    champagne

1/2 gallon chilled white wine
(Rhine or Moselle)
1 liter lemon-lime beverage
    (such as ginger ale)
Ice ring

Peel lemon in one spiral, if possible. Save the peel. In a punch bowl, mix the juice of the lemon, the sugar, and the cognac or brandy. Stir to dissolve. Chill. When ready to serve, add champagne, wine and lemon-lime beverage. Float ice ring, top with peel, and serve. Makes 15 cups.

Continental Lemonade
Zitronenlimonade

Anneliese Heider Tisdale, Cedar Rapids, Iowa

4 lemons
1/2 cup sugar
2 cups boiling water

2 cups cold water
Lemon slices

Remove yellow peel from 2 lemons in long strips. Squeeze juice from 4 lemons, resulting in about 1 cup of juice. Pour juice over peel. Stir in sugar and boiling water. Cool to room temperature. Strain into large pitcher. Mix in cold water and cover. Refrigerate until cold. Pour over ice in tall glasses. Garnish with extra lemon slices.

Kestrel Vintners wine tasting sign Leavenworth, Washington

Joan Liffring-Zug Bourret photo

Mama's Black Currant Liqueur
Johannisbeerlikör

Anneliese Heider Tisdale, Cedar Rapids, Iowa

My mother made this sweet liqueur ever since I can remember. She used to serve it after special afternoon coffees or dinners in Munich.

2 pounds plus 1 cup black
currants
6 to 8 whole allspice
1 liter 90 to 95% alcohol

(I use Everclear®)
8-1/2 cups water
7-1/2 cups sugar

Wash and stem currants and put in a strainer to dry. Place currants and the whole allspice into a 1-gallon, wide-mouth jar or non-metal container. Pour the alcohol over. Put the lid on and let stand in a sunny window (or outside in the sun) for 4 to 6 weeks. After that, boil water and sugar until the sugar is dissolved. Pour the water/sugar syrup into the berry and alcohol mixture and let stand in a sunny window for another 4 weeks. Strain the mixture through a cheesecloth-lined sieve, and then pour the liqueur into sterilized bottles.

German Beverage Traditions

Coffee and tea are the beverages Germans consume the most, outranking both beer and wine. They drink coffee primarily at breakfast and at a special afternoon coffee break, but seldom by itself, or with, or after any other meal. Most Germans have an afternoon meal around 4 p.m., not unlike British tea time. Coffee is a must with pastries; it is nearly always brewed and filtered, and tends to be stronger than American coffee. Specialty coffees, often even stronger, are also served. Coffees are served with light or whipped cream. The first decaffeinated coffee, *Kaffee Hag,* was developed in Germany. Tea is popular as a beverage to go with the traditional cold, light supper. Occasionally people add a little rum to their tea, especially in the winter. Most common is black, English tea, served with a squeeze of lemon juice and sugar.

—Hannelore Bozeman

Flaming Tongs of Fire Punch
Feuerzangenbowle

Anneliese Heider Tisdale, Cedar Rapids, Iowa

This punch was made famous in a 1944 German movie by the same name. The main character was portrayed by the well-known actor Heinz Rühmann. Do not make this in a glass punch bowl as the bowl can crack. Metal tongs or a metal strainer can be used to flame the punch. This is spectacular if you turn the lights down low when you flame the punch.

2 bottles red wine
6 whole cloves
1 cinnamon stick
Strip of lemon zest (peel)
Juice from 1 lemon
Juice from 3 oranges

1 sugar cone (Zuckerhut), about 18 ounces (250 grams)
1-1/2 cups rum or cognac (high percent alcohol)
Lemon or orange slices for garnish (optional)

Heat wine, cloves, cinnamon stick, and lemon zest, but do not boil. Add lemon and orange juices. Keep hot on warming tray. Float lemon and orange slices (optional). Warm the rum. Place tongs across container with wine, and place the sugar cone on the tongs. Slowly soak the sugar cone with the warmed rum. Light the soaked sugar cone and, as it flames, gradually add the rest of the warmed rum to keep it burning (be careful—stand back). When all of sugar has melted into the punch, serve in punch cups.

Homemade Peppermint Schnapps
Pfefferminzschnaps

10 cups water
3 cups sugar

1 pint Everclear® grain alcohol
1 small bottle peppermint extract

Bring water and sugar to a boil. Simmer for 10 minutes. Cool. Add alcohol and peppermint extract. Pour into sterilized bottles and cap.